RAISING CHILDREN THAT OTHER PEOPLE LIKE TO BE AROUND

* * * * * * * * * *

Five Common Sense *Musts*
From A Father's Point of View

By
Richard E. Greenberg F4x*

*Father of Four Kids

Raising Children That Other People Like to be Around

Published by New Generation Publishing in 2013

First Edition

52105029 ¹¹/₃

www.newgeneration-publishing.com

New Generation **Publishing**

Richard E. Greenberg

For my beloved wife
JoAnn

Once, while Honi the Circlemaker was walking down the road,

he saw an old man planting a carob tree.

Honi asked him, "How many years will it take for this tree to bear fruit?"

The old man answered that it would require seventy years.

Honi said, "Are you so healthy that you will live to eat its fruit?"

The man answered,

"I found a fruitful world because my forebears planted for me.

So will I do for my children."

-- Babylonian Talmud Ta'anit 23a

TABLE OF CONTENTS

Foreword

by
Neal Halfon, M.D., MPH
Director, UCLA Center for Healthier Children, Families and Communities
Professor, Departments of Pediatrics, Health Sciences, and Policy Studies

Several years ago my friend Richard Greenberg showed me an early draft of *Raising Children*. I had just been editing an academic book on parenting, and I was researching specific parenting behaviors and their implication for child development. Frankly, I was surprised to find that Richard's book effectively addressed the same questions I had been dealing with in my own work – and did so with authority, humor, and complete accessibility for 21st century parents.

Just as children change, grow, and adapt, parents need to do the same. Many parenting books offer advice for dealing with particular issues or specific concerns, but few provide an overall strategy that is clear, effective, and easily put into action. *Raising Children* does exactly that. The book is short on rhetoric, but clear on the insights and practices that good parenting requires.

I remember wishing that I had read this book 15 or 20 years earlier, before I started on my own parenting path. It dawned on me also that this was probably the highest praise I could give any book in my area of expertise, regardless of the author's credentials.

If I had introduced Richard at a party or other social gathering, I probably would have emphasized his successful career in film and television post-production. From my academic position, I would not have seen him as an expert in child development or parenting. But I also knew that Richard had four kids and a family that everyone loved to be around. Among my group of friends, Richard is known for his big-hearted, caring, and compassionate friendship. He is easy to talk with, a great listener, and always interested in helping others get things done. All this comes through on every page of *Raising Children.*

Richard's basic point is that parents should help their children be the kind of kids that set a good example, and are fun and pleasant to be around. But that doesn't depend on cuteness or manners. Kids can and should be kind, interesting, and engaging individuals in their own right. *Raising Children* will help parents keep that end in mind for their children and achieve it as well. Moreover, the book's usefulness is not limited to any specific family configuration. We live in a world of traditional families, single parents, co-parents, and all sorts of parenting partnerships. The ideas that Richard presents will be welcomed by all of them.

As the number of young people with mental health, behavioral, and other developmental disorders has risen, research has emphasized the importance of kids' self-regulation skills. Simply put, children who develop those skills are better adjusted, happier, and more successful in a variety of pursuits. By modelling "common sense" in areas like decision-making and discipline, parents can help their kids nurture maturity and patience in themselves. Richard urges us to frame and practice parenting as a team sport. "Winning" doesn't depend on defeating anyone. It's just a matter of having goals, communicating them, and being on the same team.

Having read the book several times, I can truly say that I have gotten something new and useful with each pass. *Raising Children* will give you plenty to think about, lots of ways to practice and reflect, and a real world context that's both practical and highly illuminating.

<u>INTRODUCTION</u>

THE PUREST PLEASURE

"I don't remember who said this,
but there really are places in the heart
you don't even know exist until you love a child."

- Anne Lamott

THE PUREST PLEASURE

The ultrasound! We had been waiting three months for this day. We took our three sons with us, as this was going to be big news. JoAnn and I had already been blessed with the three boys, Aaron (15), Benjamin (12), and Coby (7), but this time we were hoping for a girl. Aaron had been born when we were twenty-six. I wouldn't ever say that he was an accident, but we weren't originally planning on having a child just two years into our marriage. Once started, we thought it made sense to bring along our second child, Benjamin, around the three-year mark, and then, as part of our desire to regroup, and to give Benjamin a chance to establish a decent foothold on his life, we waited another five years before welcoming Coby Michael. That was it. We were done. No girl.

Done.

As the next few years passed and our boys continued to grow, I watched JoAnn jump at the chance to buy gifts for our nieces and the daughters of our friends. After all, JoAnn is the "girliest" girl I know – always well put together, never harsh or rude, patient and loving at all times. I felt that the three sons were largely mine to train, but I knew she needed someone into whom she could pour her years of wisdom and womanhood. So one day I said to her, "I think we should go for the girl." She said, "You're crazy, after three boys, the odds are really against us." I said, "Let's cheat a little,", and that began a seven-month journey to and from the office of a fertility specialist who was trying to help us "get the girl". At first it was really exciting, but after seven separate months of high hopes and regular disappointment I said to her, "I think happy eggs are fertile eggs, so let's blow off the medical hoo-ha and just see what happens."

Of course, we stacked the deck again. JoAnn bought the Ovu Quick Kit and tracked all the necessary happenings. One day, while I was in a meeting with our biggest client, I got a message from my wife saying, "COME HOME NOW!!" The meeting had started at 11 a.m. and it had taken months to set up – I couldn't leave just then – this was MY presentation. When the meeting finished, at one o'clock, I sped home ready to make a baby. Afterward, I carried great apprehension about those two hours. If we had another boy, would I get the blame because of the two hour delay?

So, here we were at the obstetrician's office, sonogram underway. JoAnn was forty-two, so she'd had an amnio four weeks earlier – but this was the follow up, and this was going to be our moment of destiny. We all crowded into the room as the doctor placed gel on JoAnn's belly, and I explained the different machines to our boys, who had never seen an ultrasound. The doctor said, "Well, this baby has fine shoulders, and the brain appears to be developing quite nicely." To which I responded, "You know doctor, we're here to determine the sex of the baby." Her reply was quick and direct. "Yes, but this is my job, and I have to do it in a specific order. I will let you know when we get to the pertinent parts." "Okay," I said sheepishly, and we boys went back to joking (mostly making fun of me for being pushy with the doctor.) After a few minutes, the doctor said, "Would you look at that?" We all turned to look at the screen, on which "It's a Girl" had been typed. We erupted in tears and relief, except JoAnn, who skeptically demanded to see the genetic outcome of the amnio in order to confirm what the doctor had told us. Sure enough, it WAS a girl.

Minutes later, we walked down the hall in a happy cluster surrounding JoAnn when suddenly she stopped short, made a face, looked at us all and said, "Did you guys hear that?" None of us had heard anything. "You didn't hear a loud boom?" "No," we all replied. "Oh," she said, appearing to think deeply. "I'm surprised you didn't hear it." "It was all of you dropping a notch in status." That was the prologue to the arrival of our fourth and final child, our wonderful daughter, Emily.

Our children are named alphabetically in order of arrival. This started out accidentally with Aaron and Benjamin, and then become a "thing" with Coby, Dusty (the dog), and Emily. This alphabetizing makes it quite easy for us (and others) to remember where each of them lies in the family order — and, interestingly enough, it seems to bind the kids together in a sequence that they appreciate. Emily even thought that the first Greenberg grandchild's name would have to begin with an "F."

As our first-born, Aaron has always been very responsible, eager to please, and quick to help out. He has a solid sense of our family and his role as the oldest child. He has been a wonderful leader for his siblings. He was "soft" as a young child – so sensitive that his teachers would tell us he needed to toughen up. Aaron quit playing Pop Warner football because someone told him his problem was that he didn't want to "hurt the other guy" -- and Aaron agreed! Aaron went to college and has his own career today. He has as much self-confidence as a person needs. He continues to love and guide his younger siblings. He is fun-loving and musical. He pays his own bills.

Benjamin arrived three years later. He was born forty minutes after we pulled into the hospital. Our regular OB was out of town, so his young associate delivered Ben. I paid for Benjamin's birth with a credit card. As a baby, Benjamin was quiet and observant. He was easily entertained by his big brother, and was in no hurry to learn to talk – he'd simply point - say "tsa!" - and someone in the family would figure out what he wanted. We worked our way through a mild and rather common speech problem with Ben, and to this day he remains a resourceful communicator. Ben is very good at managing people, and inevitably ends up running things. When he was leaving for college he announced that he was going to be a history major. I balked. "Why not be an English major? At least you can do something with that," I said. He looked at me and irrefutably said, "Dad, History IS English, it's just stories that have already been told." Case closed. Ben majored in History. Today, like his brother Aaron, Ben is a college grad and self-sufficient.

Five years passed, and Coby Michael was born. From the very beginning Coby was a source of amusement for us all – and, once he figured out that his role was to entertain, he took to it quite comfortably and naturally. He was elected President of his elementary school, and he took the job quite seriously. Coby doesn't rock the boat, but he keeps it afloat with a quick smile, a positive attitude, and a well-honed sense of humor.

In his late teens, like his brothers, Coby had a midnight curfew. One night Aaron was having a party and phoned around 11:30 to ask if Coby could stay beyond the curfew, explaining, "If Coby goes home, this whole party is going to fall apart!" Coby's charisma is unquestionable, but it took us many years and a battery of tests, to figure out how to help him focus academically. Ultimately, Coby graduated from college and is employed and self-supporting.

AND THEN... FINALLY... THE GIRL

Since the day we brought her home, Emily has been the center of our family's attention. We'd watch her instead of watching the TV. Aaron was fifteen when Emily was born. By the time she was three, he had left for college. Benjy's job was to lift Emily in and out of her car seat, and through that experience they became best and trusting friends. When she was older, and Ben was away at college, Coby drove her to school. They had long talks about the issues of the day. Each of her brothers cherishes his special relationship with Emily, and, now that she's leaving for college, our kids are as united as ever. "The Brothers" always tell us how special and smart Emily is -- and we have to agree – but from our point of view, they are all equally wonderful and entertaining.

Just as families can be populated by a wide variety of children - three boys and a girl or three girls and a boy or a thousand other combinations - there are also many different variations of parents. Some parents are single, some divorced, others are raising children in literally dozens of possible family configurations. But, in line with Ernest Hemingway's famous advice to aspiring authors, my purpose here is to "write about what I know." I obviously don't know everything, and there's definitely a lot I don't know. But I have had experiences as a parent (and observer) that I feel are worth sharing, and that I believe can be helpful even to families that may be very different from my own.

Much of what you will read in this book is "situational." Whether you're a single parent, parenting with a partner, or married with a family like mine, the role we fulfill as parents is the same in the lives of all of our children. That's our job, and none of us is going to do it perfectly. But we don't need to do it perfectly. We just need to do it well enough, and there are lots of ways to accomplish that. By telling the story of the evolution of JoAnn's and my parenting philosophy, my objective is to help you create your own. This does not mean your system has to look like mine. Every parent is different, just as everyone's children are different.

What will your daily routine look like? When should you call the doctor when your baby has a cold? How will you, your spouse, co-parent, teammate, wingman, or whatever you choose to call that person, support each other? As a single parent, what people or information can you call upon to help you keep your bearings? How can you offer and receive non-judgmental, constructive, and loving communication in order to improve and adjust your parenting template and stay on course?

I am of necessity writing from a male point of view. I hope my thoughts will resonate with fathers while also giving female readers a window into the male psyche. I bring my clearly masculine perspective to the process as JoAnn and I continue to parent on a daily basis. In general terms, this "maleness" means that I'm a little less concerned with our children's feelings, and a lot more concerned with their behavior. That doesn't mean that I don't avoid hurting their feelings. It means that I don't care whether they feel like going to bed or not. This has changed as our children have gotten older and behavior is no longer an issue, but I was never really concerned about how my three-year old felt about having to take some medicine, for example. It was just going to happen, tantrums notwithstanding.

I want to emphasize attitude and approach as well as tactics. At critical moments, parents need to pull back from the distraction of an immediate problem and discover what we really feel about the situation and what action (if any) we want to take. The overarching message is to trust your intuition, use common sense, and learn from your own experiences as a child and a parent. Use your parenting partner, or take time on your own to reflect, modify, and improve your decisions. Discuss the day-to-day, keep an open mind, and always work to improve the team.

The bottom line is this: your children need guidance, and you're the person to help them. Furthermore, they *want* you to help them, to take the lead and teach them how to navigate the world.

CHAPTER ONE

THE BACKSTORY

"Insanity is hereditary, you get it from your children."

- Sam Levenson

THE BACKSTORY

One day, when Aaron was about three or four years old, he and I set about washing my two-door Fiat while JoAnn was running some errands. The car had just enough room in the back for a car seat. Aaron was like me at his age. He wanted to be inside near the steering wheel, radio, and keys, so he climbed into the car while I put up the windows, closed the door, and started hosing off the car.

It was a beautiful warm day in Southern California and we were having a ton of fun. Aaron would put his hand on the window and I'd spray where his hand was. He'd put his face to the glass and I'd spray his face. Funny stuff. He jokingly pushed down the door lock, and I mimed how funny that was. I also indicated that he should unlock it, but he was already turning and jumping like a chimp on the seat. Oh was it fun -- until Aaron went to his car seat, and to my surprise buckled himself in!

Aaron looked at me for a moment and then he realized he was stuck. He started to cry. I successfully calmed him down, but I couldn't help but notice that the sun was now shining directly into the car, turning it into a sauna, illuminating the beading sweat on his little nose.

Through the closed windows, I tried to tell Aaron how to press the buckle so that the car seat latch would release, but, alas, it was, in fact, childproof. With his little face getting red and sweaty. I knew that time was not on my side. Since JoAnn had the other key to the car, there was only one thing I could do. I went into the house, got my hammer, and smashed the driver's side window in order to reach in and unlock the door.

I pulled him out. Life was good, and that adventure cost me a hundred and seventy five bucks.

When I told JoAnn about it, she didn't criticize me for letting him run free in the car with the keys inside. She just shook her head and laughed with me – as she did when I lost Emily skiing, accidentally hit Benjy on the head with a baseball bat, forgot to pick Aaron up from Sunday School, and any number of other things that may have happened along the way.

I realize that there are elements of this story that are specific to our cultural, geographical, psychological, and socioeconomic setting. But I also believe the real essentials of the story -- No panic, no anger, and an ability to laugh at ourselves -- cut across all boundaries. As parents we may not all be in the same boat, but we're all on the same ocean.

My mother used to say, "Don't be so open-minded that your brains fall out." Parenting is decision-making -- thousands upon thousands of decisions. What I call common sense is just the most reliable compass for guiding your decisions. Trusting in common sense solutions will help you respond calmly and effectively when raw emotion might cause unprepared parents to panic

Daniel Kahneman, who won a Nobel Prize in economics, discussed different modes of decision making in his book *Thinking Fast and Slow*. "Slow thinking" means giving things real consideration. "Fast thinking means making decisions quickly with the information at hand. My objective in this book is to offer a framework for the reflective, deeper thinking that is crucial to stabilizing the "fast thinking" and reactive parts of our parenting experiences.

When Aaron was born, I didn't feel the least bit prepared to be a parent. I was twenty-six years old, two years married to my elementary school sweetheart, and I'd never held a baby in my life. But there I was, moving my piano out of the creative space that used to be my office in order to turn it into the nursery.

JoAnn was, and is, a natural. We knew we wanted to be parents someday, but neither of us had planned to have a baby so early in our lives. JoAnn, however, had gotten her Masters Degree in Special Education and was teaching full-time for L.A. City Schools, so she was prepared on that front. I was working as a carpenter/electrician/still photographer on one of ten scheduled ultra low-budget feature films. So I, in fact, was clueless.

During the pregnancy, JoAnn went through some crazy stuff (see: crying in the bathroom for no apparent reason) and then we had Aaron. Holy mackerel, suddenly I was a dad.

Aaron is well over thirty now, and as I've reflected on my parenting experience, it turns out that parenting can be done in a number of different ways. It didn't matter whether JoAnn and I were "on course" with any specific method. It only mattered that we had some understanding of our own long-term expectations for the way we wanted to raise our children – and a willingness to accept that we were going to be doing it together. We also knew that, minimally, we wanted our children to be well behaved and respectful, as we had been taught to be.

After observing many children and many parents, it has become very clear to me that a solid set of common sense "parenting values" allowed JoAnn and me to check our progress, follow our course, see the big picture, and even maintain our sanity. Those values -- as well as an openness to learning, to being flexible, and to sharing in the process -- became the firm foundation on which we could stand while dealing with the challenges of parenthood.

DISTRACTIONS

We all have the ability to be great parents, but lots of distractions can get in the way. We all have anxiety about the uncertainties of the world today. In the past there was plenty to worry about, but at least the responsibilities associated with teaching children how to navigate the present and the future were rather clearly laid out.

Those old guidelines have given way to a new set of circumstances. The sands are continually shifting. Families are more complicated and, ironically, people are more isolated. Books have become digital files, homework is done online, cell phones and texting allow for instant communication. The best and worst of humanity, worldwide, is on display in various forms of media every day and every night.

I have spent the last decade examining the ways in which many different people, including my wife and me, approach the process of parenting, and I've concluded that the core values of the parents seem to embed themselves in the children. This has confirmed for us that our collaborative parenting method has yielded wonderful results. After repeated requests for "our secret" – and given the fact that our children tell me that I'm a "freak" about efficiency -- I set about analyzing the elements of our parenting process that have resulted in the non-spoiled, respectful, resilient, responsive, adaptive, expressive, and comfortable children that we have.

Of course, you'd expect me to say that. People sometimes tell us how lucky we were to get "those" children. Yes, part of it might be luck, but it also takes a lot of work. So we put together a "game plan."

BATTER UP

JoAnn and I think of parenting as a team sport. We began working together to meet our parenting objectives, and to motivate and manage our "players." We were doubles partners, covering each other's weaknesses and discussing strategy. At the same time we were cheerleaders, guiding our children in the directions we thought would best serve the development of our family, which was the whole team.

At the beginning, of course, we were rookies. We spent a lot of time talking about what we wanted to do as parents, wading into the unknown with only our shared, and blind, confidence to carry us. Thirty-two years and four children later, we have seen just about every play in the book, both by coaching our children and by observing the techniques of others.

Raising children requires regular examination of how things are and how we'd like them to be. The key is taking the time to discuss, reflect, and adjust. It means observing what works, and then using it. It's watching and discussing the "game films," even if they're only our best recollection of events. This helps prepare for whatever happens tomorrow or the next day. We see how our children reacted to situations and circumstances and, more importantly, it leads us to understanding how we felt ourselves.

Understanding and relying on each other gives us a "no need to panic" confidence that is at the core of helping our children learn to live responsive, calm, and loving lives. Parenting isn't easy, especially when you're in the thick of it – but we have learned that there are ways in which we can make it easier on ourselves.

I'm essentially a loving, results-oriented, bottom-liner. With the help of JoAnn's patience, good sense, sweet ways, and Masters Degree, we have created an environment in which our children always know where they stand. They know we love them, they know we care about them, and they know we love, respect and care about each other. These have become the core values of our family.

LIFE'S GREATEST PRESSURE... AND PLEASURE

Over the years JoAnn and I have shared the majority of our parenting decisions and have provided each other with loving and often humorous critiques regarding our effectiveness. As our children have gotten older, they've very cleverly (and in good humor) offered little critiques of their own. Our kids recognize us as individuals -- but they also know we're a team. We've always been very conscious of how we treat each other, especially in front of our children. We're not perfect, but we know that demonstrating our mutual love and respect for each other has served as an example to our children that they can feel in their bones.

There is no question that my life's greatest pleasure has been my family. I have never seen my children as a burden, and they have never strayed into self-destructive behavior. I avoid allowing myself to buy into old-fashioned stereotypes like thinking of my kids or my wife as a "ball and chain" or feeling that they limit me in any way. They've taught me to maintain an open, loving, and mutually respectful relationship with all of them – while still taking time to indulge my need for Sunday softball and boys night out.

You can establish the same kinds of relationships in your family. Teach through example and guide your children toward good citizenship and self-reliance. Remember that the community in which you live is a big part of the coaching staff. Understanding the behavior of people at the market, or in the drugstore, or at Thanksgiving dinner, offers our children guidance in how "adults" behave. By demonstrating your own trust, warmth, and familiarity with those people, you extend the feeling of safety and family into your child's entire environment.

Yes, sometimes this can seem like a tall order, and it *is* a tall order. The comforting fact is that we're not the first ones trying to fill that order:

- Our species has been reproducing for thousands of years.
- Many of us grew up without car seats, crib monitors, and Diaper Genies.
- In every generation there have been proud parents and beloved children.
- There has been hardship, disease, and conflict throughout the centuries – and yet, here we are!
- We are but the "now" in the long timeline of human evolution.

Those constants mean that the basic parenting process is designed to succeed. Taking it a step further, it occurs to me that parenting is an amazing opportunity to improve our species, and to teach our children how to steer themselves through the world that lies before them. That seems like an interesting and meaningful challenge, doesn't it?

Parenting is a practice, an ongoing set of experiences that we apply to a "learning system." This is a dynamic system that JoAnn and I are still developing and refining as it moves along.

All of us have developed systems and procedures in our lives. We know how to go to the market; we grab a cart, identify and select items, go to the checkout line, pay, and leave. We know the system at most restaurants. We're seated, we order drinks, the waiter takes our order, and so forth. These systems adjust and "evolve" every time we go to a new restaurant or a different market – but the behavioral template remains the same.

SENSITIVE AND SYMPATHETIC....BUT...

Although I am sensitive and sympathetic to our children, I've found over the years that I have a more direct approach to problem solving than my wife does. This is both good and bad. It's good when I hold my children accountable and am unwilling to listen to excuses; it's bad when I should have listened to their excuse and given them a break.

JoAnn has infinite patience, which I consider mostly good -- but also a little bad. She can discuss the same issue with the children over and over, covering every nuance and detailing every scenario. That's great, but when they don't return my tools, there's really very little to discuss. I have also found that the pragmatism of my "maleness" is a very good counterbalance to the vulnerability of JoAnn's sensitivity. We offset each other in a way that softens me and also increases JoAnn's resolve. Lately, I just find myself yelling "Cut the cord!" as I overhear my beloved wife discussing laundry or home furnishings with Aaron (who hasn't lived at home for ten years).

No matter what, while they're under our roofs, we are in control of the team. We are the managers. Yes, we are even the "bosses" of our children. That's because they need us more than we need them until they show us that they are capable of navigating on their own.

When traveling on an airplane, one of the regular admonitions in the pre-flight speech concerns people flying with children: "When traveling with young children, put YOUR oxygen mask on BEFORE applying the mask of your child."

There is a reason for this, and that reason is the essence of our philosophy. If you lose consciousness before your resistant child allows the mask to be put on his or her face, then you're both in big trouble. JoAnn and I have learned that taking care of ourselves, watching the "game films" together, reviewing our strategy – "Did that work? Did I goof?" -- and valuing the importance of our leadership roles are the most beneficial things we can do for our kids.

The keys to a functional system include having both specific goals and the flexibility to understand that situations and people do change. Children have their own personalities, and parents aren't perfect. Our goal has been to raise respectful, responsive, and resilient children -- individuals who understand that they are participants in the world, with a responsibility to give as much as they take. To us, responsibility means having the ability to respond, and our job has been to give our kids that ability under a variety of circumstances -- bad teachers, mean kids, "unfairness," whatever. From the beginning, we have had a very general plan: "Let's raise our kids to be people that we, and others, like to be around."

So let's keep it simple: Good parents raise their children so that, when the day inevitably comes for the children to leave the nest, they are able to fly, deal with bad weather, appreciate the sunlight, and chart his or her own journey. JoAnn and I know our children will always be part of our lives, but today our pleasure is derived by enjoying them as adults, wonderful adults who share our values, our humor, our history and our hopes.

"S.M.A.R.T."

The book is structured around five simple principles for which I have had the audacity to create the anagram "S.M.A.R.T." There are five letters so that they can be counted on one hand, and I used the word SMART because it's positive and easy to remember. The principles are the most important behaviors that influence the way our children see us – and, as they become adults, the way they see themselves.

As parents, our job is to:

Set an example.
Make the rules.
Apply the rules.
Respect ourselves.
Teach in all things.

Children make us life-long learners – not only by sharing the events of their lives, but also by keeping us in touch with ourselves, the things we believe in, and the ways we react to those events.

The book describes a process, referencing anecdotal information that affirms or teaches a specific lesson, regardless of the age of the child. There is no doubt that many of our children's adult strengths are the result of lessons learned when they were toddlers. With some solid concentration in the first few years, you can set yourself up for a very pleasurable life-long parenting experience. After all, if you pour the right foundation, and create some solid scaffolding, the buildings you build are going to stand up to almost any storm.

Everyone is capable of creating a wonderful family. "We made them from scratch," we say to each other, and this book is the closest I can come to giving you our recipe.

For JoAnn and me, it sometimes seems as though every minute we have is devoted to our children. But after all the teacher conferences, sporting events, carpooling, and homework supervising, the loving memories seem too fleeting. As we look back on all those years, we can barely remember many of the details because, as JoAnn says, "The days crawl, and the years fly by." So hold on and have fun!

CHAPTER ONE SUMMARY

Things to remember:

- Parenting is decision-making for and with children. The most reliable compass for guiding your decisions is common sense. It's the ability, or at least the intention, to see the demands of any given moment within the context of the larger goals for our kids, our families, and ourselves.
- Remember that kids, parents, and circumstances can change – and sometimes change radically. Be focused but be flexible.
- We need to accept the responsibility for making decisions. Our children's love for us will not increase if we let them decide when to go to bed. They will just begin to wonder about our qualifications as a parent.
- As parents, we must give up the need to feel good about ourselves all the time. There will be times – lots of times – when the correct decision brings moments of unhappiness to us and our kids.
- FIVE / FIVE / TWENTY - When a hard decision needs to be made, remember this formula: "For five minutes they'll be angry at you. In five days they'll forget about it. In twenty years they'll thank you."

CHAPTER TWO

SET AN EXAMPLE

"Young people need role models, not critics."

- John Wooden

SET AN EXAMPLE

Setting an example as a parent is not easy. It means we have to cross at crosswalks, it means we have to limit a tendency to swear, it means we have to put the cart back at the market and much, much more. It means taking responsibility as parents, and using the tools we already have in place that allow us to set a positive, informed, and loving example for our children. When the time comes that our children leave the nest, the most important things they take with them will not be in boxes. What they have learned will be the result of the way we, as parents, have treated each other, navigated the world, and shared our lessons.

First and foremost is the fact that whether married, single, co-parenting, or active in another sort of parenting partnership we have to respect the person with whom we share the job. Here's a perspective I've found helpful.

THE "SHARED ADVENTURE"

A newlywed friend of ours, who had been a bachelor most of his life and was quite used to being the boss, recently announced to JoAnn and me that he and his wife were going to have a baby. We were ecstatic about it, but it did get me thinking about what types of changes would be coming their way. To start, there would be the need for increased patience, flexibility and emotional generosity.

Would a man used to getting his way at work be able to surrender control? How were he and his wife going to deal with sharing tasks? Who was going to be right and who was going to be wrong? How could they make positive communication a habit and avoid criticizing each other? Their objective must be to make the baby a project that would bring them together rather than drive them apart.

When JoAnn and I started to discuss this, we recounted some of our experiences as new parents. Even though JoAnn had experience as a teacher, I saw that in raising our own actual child our mutual common sense would need to be our guide.

First, we had to accept and embrace our rookie status. As rookies, we could look at each event as a new adventure. Changing a diaper, cleaning an umbilical cord, putting the baby in and out of the car seat -- these were entirely new experiences to be shared, discussed, and dissected in a loving and mutually helpful way. We were both equally interested in pleasing each other and protecting the baby. So accepting that a slip of the hand, or an accidental pinch with a buckle was "nobody's fault" made us equally responsible.

It was all a matter of trust.

The early tasks are fairly simple. The baby is either hungry, playing, tired, or asleep. In the first months there are worrisome little things; rashes, crying, maybe a cold or fever, but generally speaking we saw our job as welcoming the baby into the world and helping to make the baby comfortable. JoAnn taught me to change diapers, and I taught her how to assemble a baby swing. (Just kidding!)

However, around four months, there are actual biological changes occurring in babies that correspond with an increased awareness of something beyond the internally-focused sensory development of the child. Very simply, the baby begins to become aware of the surrounding world. As a result, this is a good time to welcome the baby into OUR world – the one that has a schedule, feeding times, sleeping times, and playing times.

As we rookies began to hit some bumps, we had to count on each other for collective intelligence and strength. It was easy to think it was Daddy's fault when the baby was crying and Daddy was the only one in the house. But, on behalf of fathers, I'd like to say it's not particularly fair. It's human nature to want things to go the way you plan, but with babies, you don't really have tight control, and you have to be ready to roll with whatever comes your way.

One of the most important things about rolling with the bumps is how we respond to these situations and how we respond to each other. This is how our children will learn to respond as well.

JoAnn recently pointed out that she has seen mothers ridicule their mates for not helping out with their children – and then seen those same mothers criticize the way their husbands dress the child or make their lunch. That's certainly no way to encourage participation. It implies that those two people are not collaborating as equals. This is a SHARED adventure. We're tied together and we both have a vague idea of where to go. We're both adults, so let's make the most of it, respect each other, and remember our roles as managers of our team. Once problems become recognizable, they can be discussed. If you feel marginalized – bring it up! If you're disengaged, bring it up! You're a rookie – how else will you learn?

The concept of the shared adventure allowed even the most ridiculous moments to bring us together.

Once, as an infant, Aaron was sleepy and listless and had a fever. The doctor gave us some liquid medicine. Unfortunately, Aaron was very determined NOT to take the medicine. We filled the dropper and, over a period of ten minutes, both JoAnn and I tried approaching him in every possible cute and innovative way. He would have none of it. When the dropper would come near, he'd clench his lips and turn his head from side to side. Although this made a nice purple horizontal line on his cheeks, we were stuck. How were we going to get the medicine into this very willful baby?

We talked about it a bit and, despite his tears and objection, we knew we had to give him the medicine. We put him on the floor and, while I held his flailing hands, arms, and legs down, JoAnn locked his head between her knees and forced the dropper between his lips.   Once she squirted the medicine into his mouth he froze, stopped crying, and made a "What the heck was that?" face.   The ordeal was over – but we were shaken by the experience. We had been pushed to an extreme we had never anticipated. We had just used our physical strength to overpower our child in order to do what was right. We stared at each other, emotionally spent.

It wasn't fun. It was a real challenge. But we both knew it was part of our job.   We had learned the extremes to which parenting would drive us, and reflecting about it, we saw it was our only option. We laugh about it now, but at the time we never thought we'd have to get physical with our children. We knew we'd done what had to be done, and that's what mattered.

As parents and partners, we have to do our best to give up our critical ways. We have to understand that the process is unpredictable, a set of lessons to be learned. We must never forget that the process has enough flexibility to allow for mistakes. What's really important is learning from those mistakes by sharing them, talking about them, and even laughing about them together.

PUT THE OLD STUFF AWAY

Blame doesn't solve anything.   For the benefit of their children, parents should concentrate instead on sharing responsibility and understanding each other, which strengthen our marriages, homes, and family.

If having a job, or being single, divorced, too old, too young, or otherwise on your own, makes you feel that being a responsible parent is different for you than for others -- fuggetaboutit! Pack those anxieties and concerns away and put them out on the curb.

There is no formula for ideal parenting. While there are lots of variations in the spectrum of family definitions, one thing that's necessary in all of them is to take responsibility for being the parent, and to evaluate the goings-on in your home and communicate about them.

When our children were young and I was working twelve hours a day, JoAnn and I used to "meet" in the bathroom during my morning shower. We'd discuss the obligations of the day (carpool, math test, karate lesson), recap strategy, discuss any lingering thoughts, and head into the day with a game plan and some idea of what we thought was going to happen. Sometimes during the day there would be occasional phone updates. In the evening, we'd recap events, discuss the kids and determine new strategies. JoAnn might say, "Benjy got a B+ on his math test. That's a big improvement. Try to say something to him about it tonight."

This would allow me to stay involved in my children's lives and have JoAnn coach me about communicating at the same time. We are very communicative.

YOU ARE THE PARENT

Children enter our families with no preconceptions, so the baggage we bring to parenting is ours alone.

When they arrive, our children don't know any other parents. All they know is that there is someone in their life who loves them consistently, feeds them, and cares for them like no one else – and that's you. Whether we're with them all day, or parts of the day, they will come to know and appreciate us as their parent: the person who never quits on them and always has their back.

The parenting process is designed to succeed. No matter which culture you choose on this planet, there are children being born and raised to live adult lives. If you ever start asking yourself if you're parenting the "right way", rest assured that there are many "right ways" and that the only judgment of your parenting will come as a result of the behavior of your children.

This is a guarantee: WE KNOW MUCH MORE THAN OUR CHILDREN DO. That's why we are the parents. We know how to behave in a restaurant. We know not to interrupt someone when they're speaking, and we know that medicine prescribed by a doctor needs to be taken. The benefit of having to wait approximately twenty years, more or less, to have children is that we, as parents, have accumulated much of the knowledge required to guide our offspring on their journeys.

DISCOVERING YOUR PARENTAL PRIORITIES

Selma Frieberg, author of *The Magic Years*, coined the expression, "The Ghost in the Nursery" to describe the latent effects of parents' relationships with their parents and how it comes to affect our relationships with our own children.

Think back to your childhood. Try to emotionally return to various happy, sad, and scary moments that you had when you were young. Try to really pinpoint the causes of those feelings. Once you have located them, ask yourself how they feel to you today. Ask yourself if those feelings affected you so deeply that they are still a component of who you are.

For example, my parents fought a lot. Having a front row seat at a contest I never wanted to watch gave me an inner desire to avoid conflict. I developed a skill for peacemaking. It is now part of who I am, and peace is part of the culture of our home.

What feelings and/or events can you remember experiencing as a child, good and bad, that may have had a long-term impact on you? A quote from Mario Cuomo, the former Governor of New York, really made an impression on me. He said, "I talk and talk and talk, and I haven't taught people in 50 years what my father taught by example in one week."

What did your parents do that you remember most positively? Were there hugs at night? Surprise trips to the ice cream store? Goofy family photos? Being rewarded with your "Heart's Desire" choice at the market where you could choose any sweetened cereal or special candy that you wanted! What makes these events so memorable?

What do you remember most about being disciplined? Was it a belt? Was it friendly persuasion? Was it time in isolation? Was it "no dessert"? Was it a slap on the wrist? What did your parents do that you remember most negatively? Did those behaviors make you frustrated and angry with them? How can you avoid repeating those mistakes?

Thinking about these things is the first step in designing your basic parenting system. What do you want your child to remember about your parenting? That you were present? That you guided them? That you lovingly and willingly shared your knowledge?

See whether you remember the times when your parents gave you their most positive feedback. Try to remember how that felt. A good grade, a sports triumph, a music, drama, or dance performance. Praise and loving encouragement, when earned, will probably be the single most effective gift you can give to your child.

Now that you've remembered how your parents communicated with you -- and you've remembered the feelings that you had -- plan to avoid or include those techniques in your own parenting. Here are some samples of the conclusions JoAnn and I came to when, at the beginning of our parenting process, we thought back to our childhoods:

- We both vowed never to say the words "because I said so" to our children. That lasted about 8 years!

- I promised myself that, despite my childhood tendency to repeat fiction as though it were fact, I would not treat my children's proclamations lightly or with scorn (as mine had been treated at the dinner table) and would instead respond with a well-rehearsed, "Is that so?" I figured I would leave it to someone else (maybe their grandparents?) to question my children's sources and credibility. Ironically, by the time my parents became grandparents, their levels of tolerance for unsubstantiated fact were much higher than during my childhood. Go figure.

- I promised that I would do my best to keep my mind open to new music and new fashion. I also promised that I would draw the line at tattoos and body piercing.

So as you and your partner prepare to head into the job of parenting the key is to harmonize your message. Clarify the values, vision, and goals that will define the system you apply as you raise your child. I have put together the following short questionnaire to help narrow down your parenting objectives and unify your message. Although I originally created this as a one-time organizational tool, I have learned that part of a successful system is the regular recalibration of parenting messages and techniques. This can be the foundation you fall back on, year after year, as you build the "emotional scaffolding" inside your children.

Consider these the rules of the sport that your team will be playing. As managers, you and your partner will have to remember to watch game films at regular intervals, to review the day, to change the plan, to hold a mirror up to each other to see if you're both still on track. If you desire, document your conclusions after reading the questionnaire and check them every once in a while to see if you're still on course. Are you avoiding the behaviors you disliked in your parents? Are you being positive with your children? Are you communicating and reflecting your thoughts regularly with your mate?

Keeping these resolutions in mind will make the process quicker and easier than having to always start at scratch. Remember, parenting is a practice, it evolves, and lessons are taught to us every day. The more we do it, the more we reflect and share, the easier it becomes – and the more proficient WE become. Sharing and defining those lessons is one of the keys to staying on course.

THE PARENT QUESTIONNAIRE

Learning to recognize how our parents influenced us may be the most effective way of preparing for the job ahead. Here are some simple questions for you to ask each other in order to better understand the emotional land mines that you and your partner might step on.

Give these questions some open-ended time and approach them in a safe and fully trusting environment. Think of this as research. Ask lots of questions of yourself and each other. Use this as an opportunity to confess and share your deepest feelings, both painful and pleasurable. Make listening as important as talking, an important point for me in my earlier days.

- What did/do you love most about your father? Your mother?
- Did you know your grandparents? What do or did you love most about them?
- In what ways do you think your parents are like their parents? In what ways do you think they are different?
- Were your parents always honest with you? Did they always tell you the truth?
- At what moment were you proudest of your father / mother?
- At what moment were you most embarrassed by your father / mother? Would you be just as embarrassed today? (Do you feel embarrassed just thinking about it? If so, feel the power of this memory!)

- Do you remember whether or not your mother was always busy? Was your father?
- What behaviors did your parents punish most severely? Do you agree with their decisions?
- What behaviors did they encourage?
- How did your parents let you know they loved you? Will you (or do you) do the same with your children?
- Did you ever really disappoint your parents? How? How did that behavior affect the way they treated you? How did your behavior or self-image change as a result?
- When did you most feel loved? Why?
- Did your family have any rituals? What was your role in them? How did your parents handle them? Were they the leaders? Did they ever let you lead? How did you feel about that?
- Who is your favorite relative? Why?
- Who is your favorite parenting role model? Why?
- What is your greatest fear about being a parent?

We all have our own stories -- and, to me, everyone's story is interesting. Essentially, these questions ask, "What makes you who you are?" Think of your own questions and add them to the list. Then decide, from this discussion, how you're going to communicate, how you're going to strengthen each other's confessed weaknesses, and protect each other from your fears. Remember those resolutions, and use them as your litmus test when you regularly recalibrate. Not everything your parents did was right or wrong. How you raise your children is finally and entirely up to you.

CREATE A CODE WORD

Once we had had our "Ghosts" conversation and figured out what we were going to learn from our own upbringings, JoAnn and I began speaking more openly and clearly as we parented. We also learned how to communicate with each other in verbal shorthand, so as to not belabor issues or argue in front of our children. To this day we rarely argue in front of our children, and we never argue *about* our children. This doesn't mean that we don't sometimes disagree about what we'd like to do as parents, it just means that we don't have those discussions within earshot of our children.

Think about that for a second. How do you feel when you see an arguing couple? Do you feel comfortable? A little embarrassed for them? Now imagine that you are a child and your parents are arguing, especially about something that concerns you, like your grades, your haircut, or a missed doctor's appointment. Whatever you might feel exactly, those aren't good feelings.

As part of our developing "system," JoAnn and I agreed that we needed a code word to indicate that this behavior was not in keeping with our systemic values. What code word can you use to signal your partner that he or she is behaving in a manner that is best stopped now, and saved for a later private discussion? We used the word "pressing" to let each know that we had gotten to the point where what we were discussing should be postponed. This, of course, requires that both sides respect the temporary delay and stop the argument. That's an exercise all by itself, and, you'll improve with practice. Ultimately, the more we dealt with little issues, the better we were able to deal with bigger ones.

KNOW YOUR GOAL

Keeping our eyes on the "big picture" is a good way to avoid getting bogged down in the "crisis du jour."

What's your big picture, your objective, your goal in parenting?

Ours is raising likeable and respectful children that other people like to be around.

The benefits of having a likeable child are:

- Your child feels good about his/her place in the world.
- Children receive positive feedback from people around them and feel good about themselves.
- They experience praise.
- Behaving responsibly and knowing the rules also gives children the foundation they need to become valued friends, spouses, co-workers, and neighbors when they become adults.

On the other side of the coin:

- Children that are disrespectful or undisciplined may get attention, but not the kind of positive attention from which happy children grow.
- A lack of discipline lets children float unattached – often causing them to feel as though "you don't care." It also increases anxiety, emotional discomfort, and "acting out."

THE STRANGE CITY ANALOGY

When I travel on business, I'm often a little tense arriving in a strange city. I am a stranger in a strange place, with no one there to guide me.

I usually get my bag and take a cab to the hotel. I eat in the hotel or go to a restaurant suggested by someone at the front desk. As I'm always a little anxious in strange surroundings, I try to reduce my anxiety by doing what's comfortable. I generally don't feel secure enough to venture out, explore the city, or learn about my new surroundings.

That's when I'm alone.

When I go to a city where a friend meets me at the airport, the whole picture changes. With a pal who is familiar with the surroundings, I am totally comfortable and inclined to go on all sorts of excursions. Now I've got a guide, someone who knows the town and exactly how to navigate the surroundings.

That's what we do for our children. We are their guides in the comfortable place known as "home." We are here to ease their anxieties, to make their lives as secure as possible by guiding them through the maze of growing up. We know the way, and it is our job to hold their hands through their journey – because, no matter how unprepared we may feel, we have lived here a long time and we do know our way around.

Put another way, if you got into a cab and asked the driver to take you to the airport, and the driver explained very nicely that he didn't know how to get there but he'd try, I don't think you'd have a very relaxed or comfortable cab ride. Well, with our children in the back seat of our cabs, it's important that they believe that we know where we're going – even if we have to fake it every once in a while!

As parents, we must be sure that our children have confidence in our leadership, and that they know when we're teaching them the local customs – like going to bed at a reasonable time, eating healthy foods, and treating others with respect – that we believe these things are good for them.

Finally, as part of our preparation, there is this important question:

WHAT'S A MOMMY OR A DADDY ANYWAY?

You are!

That's right, for our children there is no other definition for Mommy or Daddy than the ones we create. We get to write the book, set the scene, and create the characters.

Sometimes we observe friends behaving in a manner that might indicate that they are afraid that their children won't love them. This surprises me, because I honestly believe, and have observed, that children live to love their parents. If we as parents are motivated by love, concern, and positive intention in everything we do, it's hard to believe that our children won't love us. This also means it's not useful to compare ourselves to other parents. What matters is how we define our unique roles as parents of our own unique children.

You would never intentionally mistreat your child, but even parents who abuse, ignore, or torment their children have children who actually love them. Children come into the world so innocently that they translate any parenting behavior as "love." Hitting becomes loving. Yelling becomes loving. That type of parent has issues beyond the scope of this book.

What do children really want and need from their parents? The answers are strength, consistency, guidance, and love. And it is important to understand that being firm and saying "no" is a crucial part of guiding our young children.

Do you believe it's wrong to let your children cry? Are you afraid that if you do so, they won't love you? Do you believe that taking your fragile eyeglasses away from your baby will adversely affect him or her? If the baby cries, do you think it means that she loves you less?

No.

When I mentioned raising children in a "team management" way, I was addressing my belief that prioritizing our adult lives, teaching our children to align themselves with our goals and to be full participants in the family, creates a much more consistent environment than asking them to make decisions for which they are unprepared.

As much as we love our kids, our kids are here to love us. They want to please us, and they want and need to know what pleases us. The ways in which they show their love are a reflection of the way we love them. This is why it's often more important to stare into your baby's eyes than to speak on your cell-phone or text a friend. Babies, especially, need a connection, and once this loving connection's been made, it is clear to our children that our love and their behavior at a given moment are not connected. There is no contingency in our loving relationships with our children. Making that certain in their minds is a primary task of a parent.

It was not until I was about thirty-five that I learned what it meant to be loved by my father. I came home from having lunch with him, a man I had tried for many years to please. At lunch that day it became clear to me through our conversation, his acceptance of my point of view, his willingness to laugh, and his evaluation of my professional situation, that he was pleased with me as a man. He was happy to just have a conversation, share honest opinions, and crack a few jokes. I realized he loved me no matter what I was doing.

I concluded this was true because my father was listening to me the same way I often find myself listening to my kids. I enjoy them every minute, even when I'm cleaning up their messes, but then I realized that perhaps I had not made it clear to them in the same way it hadn't been made clear to me. After a little conversation with JoAnn, I went into eight-year-old Aaron's room and told him that he didn't have to worry about whether or not I loved him – ever.

I also realized that they needed to hear that I love them, even when I'm saying "NO." It has become clear to me that children believe that people who say "no" to them, care about them. Please don't let the fact that you love your child make you think that it's wrong to say "no."

Love is the greatest gift we can give our kids, and they measure it through attention, participation, shared experience, confidence and mood -- not by our ability to produce cash from our pockets (at least not for the first few years). After all, every little child loves his or her parents, regardless of the adversity of family circumstances.

On the other hand, being a father is not just about "putting in the time." A dad who is home with his child eight hours each day is not more of a dad than the traveling salesman who calls from the road at night. Each of us is capable of reflecting on and improving our parenting, and thus creating in our children a clear understanding of our intention and our actions.

At one point early in Aaron's life, JoAnn told me that if I continued spending too much time at the office, our son wouldn't know who his father was. After giving this idea a moment's thought, I somewhat defensively replied, "He'll know who his father is, 'cause I'm the only one he's got!"

Nonetheless, it was equally important that I listen to her comment about spending more time with Aaron. I was reminded of the cliché, "No one on his deathbed ever regretted spending too little time at the office." It occurred to me that what matters to kids is having someone really pay attention to them, lead them, engage them, and take them seriously. JoAnn once pointed out to me that a good way to let them know you're interested is to drop to a knee and look them in the eye. It seems easy enough, and it works. Give it a try.

With my own children, I needed to actively pursue opportunities to spend time together. I need to create moments in which I could guide them, respond to their needs, their ideas, their jokes, and to model my behavior for them in the world. Sometimes it was just important to be without their mom.

Being a parent presents us with opportunities to do things we had never even considered trying, like coaching a sport, building a birdhouse, making a dress, or going camping. This means making a personal sacrifice in order to have a shared adventure. Each of these simple activities adds one more element to our child's concept of "mother" or "father" and creates memories of shared experiences. Sometimes these experiences don't turn out exactly as we'd planned – but there will almost always be memories to laugh about. Most importantly, our children experience the way we problem-solve, deal with disappointment ("the ride is closed"), solve problems ("there's a bathroom in there"), and demonstrate that we are confident in the way that we roam the world, engage with others, and travel our own path.

In 1986, Halley's Comet came to visit the Southern California sky. The next visit would be in 2061. I won't be around but I figured my children would, so I thought I'd take them to see it. That required getting up at four in the morning, driving two hours to the desert town of Palmdale, climbing a small mountain, and then finding the comet in the sky.

At the time JoAnn and I had (only) two children, Aaron and Benjamin, seven and four respectively. After discussing the plan with me, and recognizing that four in the morning was not her best hour, JoAnn politely described the upcoming trip as a "guy" thing and decided that she was going to stay home.

I loaded the boys into the car at four that Sunday morning to meet a few friends at a designated freeway off-ramp, and headed north. The boys slept in their seats as I drove the cold and windy way to that distant and desolate stretch where we were most certainly going to see this once-in-a-lifetime phenomenon. Or twice-in-a-lifetime, if you were lucky enough to live a long life and have a father who took you to see the comet when you were little.

When we arrived it was freezing and the wind was howling so loudly I had to yell to my friends to be heard. I woke the boys and, with Aaron on foot and Benjy in my arms, we trudged up a small hill to see the famous comet with its famous tail. Both boys were bundled in heavy jackets and all of us were being blown around in the cold and dusty wind. We looked at the southern sky and searched for Halley's Comet.

Benjy started to cry. Aaron had to go to the bathroom. The wind got worse. I yelled, "There it is!!" and pointed to the south. I held each of them up -- as if getting them two feet closer would help -- and said, "See it?" They both nodded, even though I'm sure the lack of a telescope, binoculars, or a trained astronomer made our sighting suspect. That glimpse was good enough for all of us and we hustled back to the car.

As I was buckling Benjy back into his car seat I felt satisfied that I, their father, had taken my boys to see Halley's Comet and that, surely, this would be a story that they would tell their grandchildren. We celebrated by stopping at a nearby 7-11 and buying Slurpees for the long drive home.

Years later I heard nine-year-old Aaron describing the trip to a friend. He didn't remember why we'd gotten up so early. But what he did remember was that one morning his dad had awakened him and his baby brother to go for a long drive...and get a Slurpee.

There you have it. My desire to give my sons a bit of history to carry forward in their lives was memorialized as an early morning Slurpee run. They may have a completely different take on the experience, but at least we spent time together. We experienced the world. They know I did something for and with them and, someday they will be able to say that their father took them to see Halley's Comet.

Actions speak louder than words. No matter how inconvenient it may be to get up early and coach a baseball, soccer, or basketball game, it shows your child that you care. Something special happens when you try to teach your child to understand an idea like baseball. Regardless of the quality of your coaching, you'll end up with two runners on the same base, a batter hitting the ball and running to third, and a miracle catch in the outfield. It's a commitment, but it teaches your child that you care about them, and it also teaches them that you care about other people's children too.

By supporting our children in their chosen pursuits, we are making the public aware of our pride and presence in their lives. Children appreciate our attention outside the house; it tells their friends that we care and it lets them show us off. Even if they act totally embarrassed by our presence (which in no way stops me from being a proud and outspoken parent), underneath they are really happy that we've "shown up." When they're adults, they'll come back with stories of appreciation and memories of trips to get ice cream or a soda after an event. It's amazing what *they* remember and what *we* don't!

DON'T ASSUME

As adults, we tend to project our vision of life onto our children. We assume that if we don't like to eat fish, they won't like fish either, or if we're depressed because our team lost, then they should be depressed too.

But it doesn't always work that way. As adults, we have experienced many disappointments, such as unmet expectations in love, or careers, or financial insecurity.

Children haven't yet had to cope with these types of disappointment. They still have very simple expectations. In their earliest sporting seasons, children don't care whether they win or lose; their parents do. If we're upset that they lost, then they will be upset too. If we make a big deal about winning, losing will be a let-down. Beyond sports or any other specific activity, kids do notice whether Mommy or Daddy is happy or sad, and whether Mommy or Daddy is hugging them or each other. Children learn through observation and engagement. JoAnn and I recognize this as one of the values in our "system." Even if we're not aligned in our attitudes, we are able to show our children how we state our opinions, discuss them, and arrive at a conclusion respectfully and without conflict. These modeling moments reflect the core values of the parenting system that JoAnn and I applied at that time.

MINI DATA RECORDERS

The question is not whether our children are going to love us; they are born wired to do that. The question is whether we as parents can be consistent, fair and loving with each other in a way that communicates to our children that we feel the same about them. Our job is to model our relationship in a way that teaches our children to respect, love, and communicate in the same way. This is simply a matter of making each other happy, or sincerely trying to.

I've learned that I do a better job as a parent if I can disconnect from that part of me that has to be right or needs to win. My ego, the part of me that "has something to prove," has sometimes caused me to lose perspective.

For example, when playing with kids in sports or games, I find it's important to occasionally let them win. Some parents (like my father) had an ego that just wouldn't allow it even when I was very young. He thought he was doing me a favor, toughening me up. But I remember feeling hopeless and incompetent because I'd never be able to beat him at anything. As a result, I just stopped competing. My lack of confidence caused me to avoid the potential failure of

competing. I don't think that's what he had in mind –
but that's the feeling I got, and the remedy I gave
myself for those feelings.

As our children get older and the competition gets
tougher, they will expect more of a challenge from us.
But, in the early years, simple victories are the stuff of
dinner table delight: "Mommy, I beat Daddy in ping
pong today."

By the way, despite my father's heavy hand, I
fiercely loved and admired him. Although we started
playing tennis when I was eight, I didn't win a set from
him until I was in my late teens. To this day I still don't
enjoy competition – although I do enjoy winning, and I
understand that competition is a necessary evil. We
have always encouraged and supported our children in
their competitive efforts, but winning at everything
wasn't one of the values in our "system." Some of
their teams won championships, and some of their
teams lost a majority of their games. Either way, they
knew we were just there to love and watch them.

Whether the issue is succeeding in sports, or
tackling rudeness in our children, ego isn't necessary.
Although you may be the "big cheese" in your
professional environment, the rules at home can be
quite different. In most workplaces, it is important to
command respect and issue advice or instructions with
absolute confidence.

But at home, even though we want our children to
be comfortable and to count on us, we can still do that
by showing our soft spots or innocence. I've found
that by remaining open to my children and letting
them teach me I have learned many lessons about
myself. I've also observed that children know exactly

who we are and, whether we win or lose, they will love us forever -- no matter how important we, our co-workers, or our employees think we are.

Knowing that our children are hardwired to love us, and that we have an obligation to guide them with our own behavior, it's up to us to build a framework, the emotional scaffolding upon which their lives will be constructed. Our next chapter, on Making the Rules, is devoted to the creation of that scaffolding.

CHAPTER TWO SUMMARY

To best SET AN EXAMPLE...

- Create a plan by identifying your resources and examining the "ghosts in our nursery." Discuss your parenting goals.
- Think of yourselves as team managers and understand that your job is to teach your children to be responsive, adaptive, and resilient. In order for our children to become those things, we need to spend time with them and model those behaviors.
- Adapt to circumstances by consistently and continuously evaluating and updating your parenting objectives. Share what you learn from each of the little day-to-day experiments we conduct while testing new and better ways to support our children's evolution into the kinds of children we want them to become.
- Show confidence in order to decrease our children's anxiety and make them happy and comfortable. We are completely qualified to be our children's guides in the world.
- Remember that we are the definition of parents in our children's eyes and they will love us, and admire us, and want to be just like us, even if we're not at home all the time or making them fresh meals daily.
- Caring about own needs allows our children to relax, look up to us, and adapt to our world.

CHAPTER THREE

MAKE THE RULES

"Never raise your hands to your kids – it leaves your groin unprotected."

- Red Buttons

MAKE THE RULES

Once JoAnn and I had identified the kind of parents we'd like to be and how we could communicate about our progress, we began designing our own custom system for sharing our thoughts and observations, making adjustments, and demonstrating the kind of trust and communication we would like to establish with them. We also determined that children need coaches. As a result of our life experience and experiential common sense, we knew that they were not our equals on the team that is our family.

In this chapter, we will examine reasons for making rules, and why it is important for parents to establish a firm tone and a foundation of expectation, so that our children will feel our confidence and know that they are safe in our guiding hands. We will also examine ways in which parents, as co-coaches, can help each other define rules, explain them to our children, and remain strong in moments of doubt.

RULES ARE THE ARMS IN WHICH OUR CHILDREN CAN EMBRACE THEMSELVES

Just because we can make babies, we're not guaranteed to be "good" parents. To be a good parent and raise a confident, happy child we must be willing to accept the responsibilities and obligations that go with the job. This is especially true with very young children for whom guidance, supervision, and feedback equals security. Older children who have not been taught to respect their parents or other adults are not suddenly going to adhere to rules. So it's best to start defining our expectations as early in our children's lives as possible.

If I had to define the word "brat," I would say it's just a child who is in control of the parent. We cannot allow our young children to become our bosses. We cannot allow them to believe that they know what time would be best for their bedtime or whether they need to take their medicine.

Over the years, they'll resist on various fronts. But we must remember that our children don't have the credentials to override our adult logic or experience. As much as our children are gifts to us, we are gifts to them. There may come a time when your child will say, "You're not the boss of me." And there will come a time when you really aren't "the boss" of him or her. But until our children were able to prove that they were capable self-bosses, we emphatically remained the primary authority figures in their lives.

JoAnn and I often observed that children act out because they are in need of limits. Absence of limits often causes them to be uncomfortable and anxious, unable to feel secure. The first thing a baby knows is the pressure and security of the womb. This is why we swaddle newborns and keep them tightly in a cocoon of security. As they get older the cocoon expands, but it's still necessary. Rules and expectations within our home become a replacement for the embrace of tight blankets.

Think about it. Aren't you more comfortable when there is a line or a "take a number" system at the bank rather than a free-for-all with multiple lines moving at different speeds and people butting in front of you? JoAnn and I have learned that children rise to meet our expectations. So we expect the best from them.

We have always believed that rules are the arms with which our children can embrace themselves. That philosophy allowed us to understand the function and importance of diligent guidance as we began to build our parenting system. We looked at the rules we created as the nuts and bolts that would hold the whole thing together. Providing a strong internal foundation let the kids know we cared, and gave them the confidence to believe in themselves through our behavioral model and expectations.

WHAT ARE THE RULES

JoAnn and I never consciously laid out a set of rules and then tried to live by them. It wasn't like the traffic laws. Instead we just used our defined system of values and goals to organize and guide our children's behavior. In our system, wanting our children to be "good sharers," to like each other, to tell the truth, and to respect other people were the goals we created for ourselves and them. This meant that we had to invent various incentives and procedures that would lead them toward those behaviors. For example, we had rules against hitting, bad-mouthing, accusing, or complaining about their siblings. It wasn't written in a book or on a wall, it was just a behavioral expectation that we conveyed to our children.

Of course, they didn't always comply. This meant we had to continuously figure out how to implement rules in a way that would not only stop the immediate behavior but also consistently communicate our message. As this was one of our core values, we were very serious and unwavering about the issue. Wanting them to tell the truth would lead us to reward honesty and to frown upon fiction.   Misbehavior always became a teaching experience for us.

WHO'S IN CHARGE?

Everyone has a natural tendency to resist regimentation. As a college student, I was part of a generation that believed that conformity was a dirty word. Now mainstream ad campaigns carry slogans like "Think Different" that encourage us all, through both behavior and bad grammar, to avoid conformity.

As the parents of toddlers, however, we really want our children to conform. After all, adhering to society's standards for public behavior -- not screaming in public, hitting, or biting other children, saying "please" and "thank you" -- is essential to long-term success around town and in the world.

Young children aren't ready to call the shots. After all, every age group goes through a period of testing, a time when we choose not to conform and to see what happens. Certain behaviors are developmentally appropriate, and what is developmentally appropriate certainly changes as children get older. But the objective in the early years is teaching our children what we expect of them – to define what is developmentally appropriate for them – until they're capable of taking the responsibility to make behavioral decisions on their own.

Children act out because of anxiety – at least I did! Not knowing where I stood would sometimes motivate me to "push a button" and see how my parents would react. In some strange way, that reaction was reassuring.

An acquaintance of mine who recently moved from Australia to the United States described herself as suffering from "choice stress." In Australia when she went into a coffee shop and asked for coffee, that was it. Coffee was coffee. In Berkeley, her new home, she became anxious when she had to make so many decisions. What type of coffee beans? What size drink? Regular or decaf? Whole milk or non-fat? These options actually added stress to her life until she turned it into a routine.

As a person who gets nervous when asked "paper or plastic," I could completely relate to the idea of *choice stress*. When I applied it to children who are even less equipped to make decisions, I could see the attraction of a life in which choices like "dinnertime" and "lights out" are made by the parents. There is comfort, at times, in being guided. Imagine if you got into a taxi and the driver asked you which pedal was the brake. Not a real confidence builder.

MARGINS

As when they learn to write on lined paper, children need margins. As teens, they're going to want to move outside the margins just to prove they're not "children" any more. These margin tests are an important part of the child's self-discovery. How we deal with them is an important part of parenting. How we deal with these decisions should be defined by the guidelines we created in Chapter 1.

Realizing that we and our children are evolving every day, our goal is to allow the margins to change but to keep everyone on the page. Setting real and reasonable margins in the early part of our children's lives allowed us to limit rebellion as our kids moved into their teen years. We monitored their behaviors, made adjustments based on trust, and allowed more freedom as it was earned. We also made it clear that freedom was earned by behaving responsibly and demonstrating good judgment.

We've all done some stupid things and we've all known people who got themselves into wildly lame situations. Generally speaking, those of us who stayed in the margins understood our limits enough to avoid breaking the law, ruining other people's property, or doing physical harm to ourselves or others. There were also people who were truly wild, who had never learned about limits or had never experienced consequences when exceeding them. I always found it a liability to hang out with people like that, so I avoided them – and I've noticed that my children avoid them as well.

I've observed that children who never had margins set for them tended to take drastic action -- essentially leaving the page -- just to find out what limits their parents might impose. If the parents failed to impose limits, those children would do something even more drastic to get their parents' attention. Ironically, these kids want to be guided. To them, having parents say "no" means having parents who care, and having parents who allow any type of behavior means they "don't care."

When Emily was fifteen years old, she was asked to go get some ice cream by a friend who was a newly licensed driver. In California, a newly licensed sixteen-year-old driver is not legally allowed to have other kids as passengers in the car, so Emily declined. However, she suggested that her friend bring her some ice cream, which he did. When he showed up, however, he had one of her other friends with him. Emily asked her friend why she'd ride with the new driver and why her mother would allow it. Her friend said "My mother doesn't care – she doesn't love me like your mother loves you."

It's important to note that Emily was the person drawing this line, not us. As her friends began getting their driver's licenses, JoAnn and I began discussing this issue with her. Aside from its being against the law, we had learned from Emily's brothers that kids' having their peers in the car is incredibly distracting. Emily agreed and, although it was often inconvenient for us to have to go pick her up when her friends could bring her home, our part of the agreement meant we'll do what we have to do in order to help her do the right thing. By the way, some of the best conversations happen in the car on the way home from those events.

From the earliest ages, children test us. This is not just because they have a need for attention, but because they have a need for self-definition that, without adult help, is often misguided. When we give our young children positive attention – praising them when they recognize limits, making the rules clear, and explaining consequences for misbehavior -- our children will be more inclined to believe we know what's good for them, seek our help, and listen to our advice even if they don't agree.

I'm often amazed when I hear a parent ask a toddler for permission to talk to a friend or go to the bathroom. "Will it be OK for Mommy to go to the bathroom?" By giving our children this level of control, we not only engage in an unnecessary and potentially "losing" discussion, but create stress in them when they have to guide *us*. This also risks running into some real issues as they get older. It is said that the behavior we teach our children as toddlers is often magnified in their teens. In fact, the toddler years are sometimes called "The First Adolescence." If we teach our children that they're in control when they're little, imagine what will happen when they get older.

When Emily was young, she knew when it was time for bed, she knew not to feed the dog from the table, and she still managed to make up songs, play princess, and spend hours living in her own fantasies. Some people argue that a well-behaved child is the result of "repression" and limited in their individuality because they've been hammered into conformity. Discipline is not about uniforms, salutes, or clicking heels. It's about courtesy, kindness and respect for the feelings of others. It's our job as parents to teach these forms of civil engagement through our own behavior and guidance.

TANTRUMS AND THE LESSON AT THE MOON BOUNCE

Sometimes we parents just don't know what to do. This can mean that our children will be influenced by the bad behavior of other children. Once, at a school carnival, JoAnn and Emily were faced with a dilemma. It was a splendid gathering featuring clowns, face paint, Cinderella, and a Moon Bounce.

A Moon Bounce, or Bouncy House, is one of those inflatable huts in which children jump for hours, bumping from wall to wall and often careening into each other as if in some munchkin sized "mosh pit."

It's lots of fun if an adult is present to supervise the activity. The children often have to be separated into small groups by age or size and the number of children inside the moon bounce needs to be regulated to avoid overcrowding and injury.

As a 3-year-old, Emily was pretty small. She weighed about 25 pounds, so when she would go in a Moon Bounce with other kids she'd get knocked around quite a bit. Being no fool, Emily did not go in the Moon Bounce at this event until she had an opportunity to do it alone. Her opportunity arose when Cinderella decided to hold court for the rest of the children at the party. With JoAnn at her side, Emily ventured out to experience the joy of bouncing up and down in an enclosed inflatable house.

When JoAnn and Emily arrived, there was another little girl bouncing while her mother guarded the entrance. Even one other bouncer was enough to discourage Emily, so she and JoAnn took their positions as next in line. JoAnn explained, in a voice loud enough for both Emily and the nearby mother to hear, that they would just have to wait for the little girl to finish before Emily could have a turn. Following the cue, the little girl's mother began to prepare her daughter for surrendering the Moon Bounce to the next child.

However, the daughter would have none of it, and the mother didn't know what to do. Rather than announcing "two more minutes" or just urging her child to come out, the mother, fearing that her daughter would have a tantrum or worse, looked sheepishly at JoAnn as if there were nothing she could do about her daughter's behavior. JoAnn walked away and waited from afar for the Moon bounce to open up.

After what seemed like hours, the stubborn girl quit jumping and Emily got her turn. The other mother had made it clear that her child was in charge and that the potential tantrum was going to be that baby's ace. Unfortunately, this mother had communicated her lack of resolve to her daughter and, as a result, had gotten ignored (again). Parenting takes practice, and it's often not very convenient. We have to be ready to do the uncomfortable thing – and sometimes, without the proper skills or confidence, we choose to do nothing, which is the equivalent of giving our approval.

I'm sure you're thinking that this particular mother should have said, "Time's up now and we're going to give this other little girl a turn." Remember, she *did* say those things to her child, who couldn't have cared less. At that point, rather than acting as though taking turns didn't really matter, and what Mommy had just said really had no meaning, the mother should have had her yield to the next child in line even if it meant climbing into the Moon Bounce, taking her hand, and helping her leave.

Ironically, this mother's behavior only validates and strengthens the child's potential tantrum. If a behavior can embarrass you, it will certainly be used by your child to do so. Remember, this is about control. If you give your child a tool to control you, you are empowering the child to do just that!

JoAnn and I made it clear to our children, even at a very early age, that their behavior would be a reflection on them, not on us. They could kick and scream all they liked and it wasn't going to get a rise out of us. There have been occasions when we've removed our children from a situation (restaurant, market, concert), or apologized to the people near us, but we've not allowed any of our children to "win" an argument with bad behavior.

What do we do when our children engage us in a battle for control? For starters, we stay calm and try not to react with emotion. We do our best to detach their behavior from our egos. After all, we have prepared for this situation in our "system." We have determined that one of our values is to raise a respectful, well-behaved child. With this understanding, and the knowledge that everyone goes off the rails once in a while, we can observe their behavior without internalizing it.

If the situation had been reversed at the Moon Bounce, and my child was using the Bounce while another child was waiting, I would probably have gone into my "Obie Wan Kenobi" mode. As Obie does when speaking to a guard in Star Wars, I would have looked directly into Emily's eyes and said with an assured, measured, and very steady tone, "It is time to give the other child a chance to play on the Moon Bounce."

Try it. Your children will come to know and recognize this voice. They will know what it means, and they will do what you ask. Just remember that success with this technique depends on the strength of your commitment and the power of your will.

Serious is serious.

Another excellent technique, often used by JoAnn, is to warn our children by offering a reasonable ending, like "OK, two minutes left!." This provides a little more time to really soak up the experience, but it also prepares them for the eventual departure. If that fails, and they're still unable to pull themselves away, there's always "The Countdown" as in: "I'm going to count down from five, and then it will be the next little girl's turn" or "I will give you until the count of three to get your teeth brushed."

We have never actually reached three. We've hit two-and-a-half, and even two-and-three-quarters, but we've never gotten to three. To our children, three is an unimaginable, dire consequence.

If none of that works, we would just have to physically remove them from the situation. In those cases, we would demonstrate that the need to follow our instructions was primary, and our potential social concern about "What's everyone going to think about our disciplining our screaming kid?" was completely unimportant to us and redirected to our child as, "If you want to have a fit, that's your choice." Once children know we're serious about our mission, they recognize the futility of misbehaviour. Remember parent: The Force is with you!

THE TRUTH FLOATS

Parenting problems have been happening for thousands of years. Socrates said, "Children today are tyrants. They contradict their parents, gobble their food, and tyrannize their teachers." Today we see our roles as parents so greatly magnified that a simple mistake -- like calling a child by a sibling's name, doubting whether we ourselves are doing a "good job" -- can get really blown out of proportion.   (And, believe me, if it can be blown out of proportion your child will blow it out of proportion).

The key to reducing the impact of these simple errors is keeping our focus on the big picture — the long-term goals we have for our children and ourselves.   Adherence to these convictions will be tested regularly in a seemingly infinite number of ways. Whether our child is just randomly crying or really in danger, our values must guide our behavior. If we can keep our eyes on the lesson, regardless of momentary tears or anger, the long-term goal will always see us through.

In designing our personal parenting systems, our goals and intentions helped keep us grounded when our own insecurity might have thrown us off balance. If we know that what we have decided is consistent with our "slow thinking" objectives and is honestly the best decision we can make at that time, we are then able to deal with the questions or complications that inevitably arise.

When we are confident of our vision and goals, that confidence will trump any mistakes we might make along the way. In fact, the purity of our long term objectives allows us to bypass the temporary obstacles.

If you've ever tried to hold a bubble underwater with your hand, you'll note that it finds a way to squeak between your fingers. In the same way, no matter how you, your child, or someone else might question your intent, it will find a seam. The purity of your motivation works its way around the edges, managing eventually to rise to the top.

We were vacationing when we encountered an acquaintance whose child was in school with one of our sons. When we began sharing stories about our children, our friend suddenly posed the following question to me: "What do you say when your teenage child regularly accuses you of not loving her?" I thought for a moment and then asked, "Do you love her?" Our friend immediately replied, "Of course I do!"

"Then why are you letting your daughter's question rattle you? If you truly love your daughter, she will ultimately realize it. It's the truth, isn't it? Perhaps she knows that by asking whether you love her or not, she can shake your confidence and make it appear that you may not love her - which, we agree, is a ridiculous concept, but one that you accept by questioning yourself."

Little children, with whom there is less dialogue, can also make us doubt ourselves. Most of the doubt can be eliminated by having confidence in ourselves. "Did I really need to take away that stick?" (Yes !) "Is sunscreen really necessary enough to interrupt play?" (Absolutely!) With younger children, there's not a lot of need for debate, but, as they get older, they make compelling arguments.

Regarding the accusation of "not loving me," this came on the heels of getting grounded. The mother had made this decision because she was not confident that her fourteen-year old daughter would be safe if she let her go out with some new, unfamiliar friends.

Certainly, this was a far more loving act than allowing her daughter to head out into harm's way just to make the girl happy. The mother clearly loves her daughter; the daughter has just found one of her mother's buttons. Maybe someday the daughter would realize that keeping her from going out was an act of love on the part of her mom.

My objective was to help that mother see the bottom line in their relationship and to restore her confidence. Ultimately, somewhere down the road, her daughter would be grateful that her mother chose to keep her safe.

I suggested that the mother explain quite calmly to her daughter that this was an issue of judgment rather than love. The mother was going to use her best judgment -- which is more evolved than that of the daughter -- and not permit her to do something dangerous. As a loving, knowledgeable, and experienced mother, that is her job.

Further, the mother could explain that making the accusation of "non-love" was essentially a waste of their time. She would listen and consider her daughter's requests more carefully if the daughter would just be a little more direct in the future.

The truth, defined by that mother's parenting values, should have been very apparent to her daughter; it just needed to be presented in an understandable, sympathetic, and respectful way.

In older children, where patterns have been developed and parenting weaknesses have been identified, the challenges are often tougher. Everyone knows that safety is important, but telling an older child to be home by midnight, or that you don't like a certain friend, can sometimes be challenged by our children in a more subtle way. Sometimes we, as parents, can lose sight of our goal.

Conversations with our children are crucial to exposing and explaining our values in a way that allows us all -- the team managers and the players -- to evolve based on what's happening in the game.

It's important to note that we cannot do whatever we want just because it's responsive to our values in a vacuum. If the Moon Bounce mother had believed that her daughter deserved more time than the other children and felt no obligation to yield, it still wouldn't have been okay to leave everyone else standing in line. We must see our "goals and values" in context and remember that they are always relative to the environment. Each of us brings a unique perspective, with our own values based on experience. It is by constantly discussing what we want for our children that we narrow our goals down to the "absolutes" of reasonable, applicable expectations of behavior. As our children grow older it's really interesting to include them in the discussions.

This is how we make the rules.

I also believe that there are cultural issues that often need addressing. In some cultures, boys are mini-kings. Boys are encouraged to behave in ways that some of us might consider brash, entitled, and even disrespectful. As our nation is the greatest "melting pot" in the world, I also think it's important for parents to examine the environment in which they live and to try to understand the culture around them.

Recognizing our own motives allows us to be confident about our decisions. I remember my parents' saying, "Someday you'll thank me for this" as they were dropping me off at Sunday school or forcing me to go to a dance lesson. Although I objected regularly, they were doing what they thought was best for me and in retrospect, it wasn't so bad. (I'm still a reasonable hoofer.)

Sometimes we may believe that our child has misunderstood our motive. When we've taken away a toy or imposed some other seemingly harsh restriction and our child questions why (or bursts into tears) it is often necessary to remain confident while explaining our objectives and decision. One of the most positive memories I have of my father is that, despite whether he had yelled at me for some transgression, or we'd just had a disagreement, he would always seek to clarify his motive and, sometimes, apologize for losing his temper. This let me know that, although he wasn't perfect, he loved me enough to explain and was always trying his best.

As parents, we don't do this to enter into a debate. We do this to inform our "students." Ultimately, our objective will carry the day. We will have done the right thing, regardless of what our child says.

Once our son Benjamin was placed in a class with many of his friends, but with a teacher we knew to be very wrong for Ben. We had learned from an experience with Aaron, that this particular teacher was unlikely to impose the sort of discipline that we felt Benjy required.

After much lobbying with the school, and a tearful conversation with Ben, we changed his class. He felt that moving him from his friends would ruin his life, but we held firm to our belief that we had made the right decision. What later occurred confirmed that fact. First, none of Benjy's friends abandoned him. Next, he began to flourish in his new, more structured, class environment.

Carrying and sharing the confidence that is defined by our long-term goals gives us the perspective necessary to avoid minor skirmishes and wasting time in pointless conflict. A friend of mine recently told me that her husband has a tendency to argue fervently with their seven-year-old daughter about whether or not it is time for bed. All I could do was tell her the story of the Gorillas.

GORILLA LOGIC

There is always a dominant male gorilla in a pack of gorillas. He is the strongest, oldest, and most powerful of all the males in the group. With some regularity, younger gorillas physically challenge his sovereignty.

They swipe at him with their paws, growl, and show their teeth with menacing ferocity.

The bull gorilla growls back and even engages in some serious tussling until the fun wears off and he tires of the challenge. At that moment he puts his large and powerful hand on the shoulder of the most aggressive younger gorilla and looks him in the eye, communicating one simple thought: "We are done now. You will not be happy if this goes any farther." The younger gorilla understands that the "game" is over and respectfully resumes his position in the pack.

A boss to whom I was once complaining told me this story when I whined on about a lower-ranked co-worker. "Why even bother to engage with him?" he asked, "You're the boss – be the big gorilla."

We parents are the big gorillas. Of course, we're not going to harm our children, but it is our duty to avoid engaging with them on issues when we know we are correct. Does it make sense for a thirty-five-year-old adult to argue with a seven-year-old child?

Know your position and make your decisions with confidence. Decisions that we as parents make in the best interests of our children will always stand the test of time.

Our children used to tell us that "Susie's parents let her stay up 'til midnight." We'd respond with quiet resolve: "That's how they do it in Susie's family, but not ours." Surprisingly, that answer was quite adequate for all of our children.

CHAPTER THREE SUMMARY

When MAKING THE RULES...

- It's crucial to have a personalized parenting system, from which we are able to define a set of expectations, and preferred behaviors (rules) that unify us as a team and a family.
- Our decisions must come from a unified place, giving our children a stable and secure environment, and reducing their anxiety.
- We must recognize that we reduce our children's anxiety by having clear boundaries and expectations.
- Revert to "slow thinking," and use and teach those rules in order to make parenting easier.
- "Check in" with each other and reflect about your parenting behaviour, because the "system" becomes more natural, and keeps us from drifting too far from our long-term goals.
- It is important to recognize our own vulnerabilities and enjoy the process - laughing through the lessons we are learning together. By continuing this communication, we can adapt to change, be more resilient, and bounce back from the regular challenges and "mistakes" we sometimes learn we've made.
- Be HONEST about your hunches and feelings.

CHAPTER FOUR

APPLY THE RULES

"If you want to recapture your youth,
just cut off his allowance."

- Al Bernstein

APPLY THE RULES

This chapter focuses on attitudes which can help grow a continuing relationship of love and respect with our children, and illustrates some situations wherein better decisions could have been made. We'll also look at ways in which we, as parents, can keep our focus on applying rules when there are many ways to be led off course.

PLEASE NOTE: Parents dealing with the demands of newborns and infants may wonder why some of these stories (about older children) are applicable to them. But the examples in this chapter reflect the importance of building that "Emotional Scaffolding" when our children are quite young.

DO IT EARLY

Here's a fact: I started my parenting process as a pretty rigid person. I had been raised by some strict people whose philosophy was simply "my way or the highway." I also felt that if JoAnn and I didn't teach our children to respect and obey our rules, they wouldn't obey anyone else's. This was a pretty operable attitude for both of us in their early years, but as I mellowed and our children were showing greater responsibility, we made occasional exceptions: "OK, you can watch TV even though it's a school night".

The children appreciated our flexibility and, on a few occasions, even thanked us for it. By our system's standards, they had earned their increased freedom. And we told them so, in order to further reinforce their good behavior.

The rules we create to teach our lessons aren't all cast in stone. They are guidelines that simplify our lives and relationships. At a certain point, they become second-nature, and if our children learn them early it makes life downstream a lot easier.

As children get older they discover all our soft spots and specialize in revealing them at every opportunity. For this reason, it's important to define and impose structure on them while they are still young, impressionable, and willing.

With young children, it's easiest to fall back on a precedent, saying to your six-year-old, "I'm sorry, 8:00 is your bedtime and that's just the way it goes." If pressed further, you might offer some explanation: "If you stay up any later, you'll be crabby all day tomorrow and neither of us wants that to happen."

The problem with offering an explanation is that you're opening the door to a discussion. Frankly, if 8:00 is bedtime, there is really nothing more to discuss. I don't mean to squelch my child's idealism, or deny my child a voice, I just don't want a prolonged conversation to become a diversion from the need to go to bed. Yes, they will try that. After a bit of this, you may choose to avoid the discussion and just explain that "bedtime is bedtime." If you remain consistent, my bet is that you'll find your children will go to brush their teeth and take comfort in knowing the routine.

Think about being a new driver. When we were taught to drive, we were expected to know and follow every rule. We came to complete stops at stop signs, we always looked over our shoulders, we carefully checked both mirrors, and regularly signaled before lane changes.

As the years passed, and we got more comfortable behind the wheel, we began to improvise a little. The rules became second-nature and, although we weren't following them to the "T" anymore, we knew what they were and we stayed within the limits defined by our desire to be responsible. As parents, our job is to first teach our kids the rules (basics – like following instructions), and then supervise the way they behave on the road (allowing them to earn more privileges). When they're little, we're the Driving Examiner. We're making sure that they remember all the rules and are doing their best to be model citizens.

It's a good idea to start out a bit more rigid than you actually want to be. In the early years, it's important to be the cop. It's hard at first, so JoAnn and I would regularly discuss the challenges and give each other strength to hold strong. In the end consistency will become your friend and your children will begin to anticipate your messages without pushing the limits every time. For years, at 9:30 we would yell,

"Coby!" He would reply, "I know, bedtime." Logical rules and consistency are the keys.

IN THE BEGINNING

With infants and toddlers, we boiled down our first basic rules from these three questions:

- Is it safe?
- Will this create a habit?
- Does this make sense to me/us?

BASIC RULE ONE: Is it safe? - This one's pretty easy. Don't touch wall sockets, don't put dirty things in your mouth (and don't leave them lying around), don't touch the stove, don't go out the back gate or the front door. Children catch on pretty quickly to these, especially if you drop to a knee, use a "special" voice and look them in the eye when you tell them something is dangerous or a "no no."

Doing our part as parents is important too. We put all of our dangerous or fragile things (chemicals, crystal, fancy knick-knacks) out of reach of our little children and generally "baby-proofed" our house (plugged our electrical sockets, put clips on drawers) Beyond that, with the exception of a gate at the stairs, we didn't put padding on our coffee tables or alter our physical environment. Learning to navigate our house, edges and all, was also our children's responsibility. They learned from us not to touch the stove or run where they might slip, and it encouraged them to be careful on their own.

BASIC RULE TWO: Will this create a habit? – This one's a little tougher. The rule is more about our behavior than that of our children. Everything we do as parents can become an expectation on the part of our children. If we leave their light on for two nights when we put them to bed, they'll expect the light to be left on forever. If we let them sleep in our bed for two nights in a row, then you can be sure that they'll want to toddle their way into the bedroom on night numbers three, four, five, and forever. It's especially important in this instance to weigh your glorious pleasure -- at having this wonderful, warm, sleeping angel next to you --against the fact that it's not going to be particularly wonderful to have your child wanting to join you in bed whenever they want.

I know there is a movement today toward "Attachment Parenting" -- but, seriously, from the male point of view, this is a biggie. I consider our bed to be a private place for JoAnn and me – a refuge for the original relationship that led to having those wonderful, but not-in-my-bed, children. There are many differing opinions on this issue, and it's really up to you and your spouse to determine how you plan to deal with this. In my case, I am rarely happy when one of my children is not only taking up my space in bed, but also distracting JoAnn from her original bedmate - ME. That's why our children have their own beds.

BASIC RULE THREE: Does this make sense to me/us? JoAnn and I will usually have decided whether or not it's alright for our kid to play in a puddle, eat a dog biscuit, or bang on the kitchen pans. Everybody makes their own decisions about these sorts of things, and you'll probably learn that some of your friends are crazy, but whether you let your dog lick your baby's mouth, or whether your kids play without their clothes on (in the privacy of your home) is entirely up to you.

I grew up in a house where there were a lot of odd "rules" – which, I suppose made sense to my parents. One of them was Eating Everything On Your Plate, another was Making Your Bed, another was Absolutely No Sugared Cereals, and finally, No Soft Drinks. These rules, especially cleaning one's plate, made every meal a trial with potential conflict. Although we are structured in our parenting, which some might regard as "strict," we've got plenty of room in our house for fun – starting with not creating things to argue over. If our children didn't make their beds, they returned to their own messy rooms. If they didn't eat everything on their plates and they got hungry later, it was their problem to feed themselves. We continue to teach them to avoid worrying about things we can't control (like telephone lines near the house), and we try not to bring the fears of the world into our home (like discussing money problems, or serious health issues, in front of our children). But that's just us, and that's what we agreed to in our plan.

CONSISTENCY

Consistency is something I experienced while growing up. My parents held firm on many things when I was little, so that these things would become part of my character. I had to tell the truth and I had to be respectful, which meant doing as I was told.

JoAnn and I also chose to believe there is value in remaining consistent in our positions.

As a ten-year-old, I once had a friend over to play. We had decided to ride our bikes out of the area approved by my parents and I went to ask my mother for permission. She said no. I came back into my room and my friend asked me what she'd said. When I told him that she had said no, he encouraged me to go back to her and ask her again, only this time with some urgency and a sense of pleading, which had always worked on his mother.

I explained to him that once my mother made a decision, she never changed her mind. It wasn't even worth the trip back into her bedroom. My mother was consistent, but not unreasonable.

As I've gotten older, managing both a family and a business, I have understood the value of policy and the need for consistency. Rules are essential. You can always make a decision to alter a rule, but alterations should be earned and respected as exceptions. We're also able to use rules to protect our children from risks that they may not perceive.

JoAnn and I live walking distance from the local elementary school, and we established a rule that our children had to tell us whenever they were going up to the school for any reason. In fact, they had to tell us where they were going whenever they left the house. If they broke that rule, they weren't allowed to leave the house for a day or so. I don't remember any of them actually breaking that rule. For kids living at home, that "reporting" of their plans and whereabouts continues to this day. Even our college graduate son, Coby (who spent four years living outside our home), lets us know where he plans to be and when he can be expected home – which is now more of a courtesy than a rule. Cell phones make this much easier.

IT'S EASIER TO LIGHTEN UP THAN TO TIGHTEN UP

We will always need to make exceptions, but we need to be very careful when doing so. Being too flexible too early allows children to believe that "rules are made to be broken," and that's no way to keep order in your house. Young children are open to guidance and discipline, but a child who has experienced loose parenting can become a real problem when by around age eight or nine. Suddenly, a physically bigger child's misbehavior or backtalk is more forceful, publicly embarrassing, and harder to explain. At this point, formerly undisciplined parents may futilely begin to try imposing restrictions on their children. Those parents have created what I call "upside down children."

At eight or ten years old, the upside down child has developed behaviors that impede a parent's ability to guide and govern. Rudeness and disrespect often arise, leading to incredible frustration, power struggles, and communication problems. These situations often require professional help, as the communication path between these children and their parents has been trampled in one direction or the other. In many cases, the parents need strength from an outside authority. This is why, as parents of young children, it's important to start out firmly, establishing your rules and values as early as possible.

If you have established the rules, then regular parental re-examination can lead to an appropriate "lightening up." A couple of weeks after my mother had denied us the freedom to ride our bikes outside of the "approved" area, my friend came over to play again. My mom called me into her bedroom and explained that she had overheard what I had said to my friend the last time, thought it over a while, and decided that I was now responsible enough for her to move my biking border out a little bit farther. She reminded me to be very careful, because I'd be riding my bike in new "shark-infested waters," and sent us on our way.

My friend and I had a really fun afternoon and returned quite safely later in the day. It was a unique exception on the part of my mother, perhaps the first, and that must be why I remember it. I had earned her respect enough to ride farther – something I remember fifty years later.

MAKING EXCUSES FOR YOUR CHILD

JoAnn and I observed that when parents excuse their infants' bad behavior with phrases like "he was born that way" or "she just hates to sit still" they generally end up with a lifetime of lame excuses as their children grow older, like "his teacher hates kids with red hair" or "she accidentally put that candy in her purse, she wasn't stealing it!"

This pattern can begin very early. It can start in the crib when we put our children down "for the night." If they cry, and we check the diaper, make sure they've had a good burp, and that no part of their clothing is scratching them, then all systems appear to be "go" for a good night's sleep.

But wait, the hall light is on...or not...and their little froggy plush is scaring them because it has a blue eye, and the baby hates the fact that the froggy has only one blue eye...or our music is too loud...or they miss us...

You get the idea, right? We can always create reasons that excuse our children from doing what's expected of them, which, in this case, is sleeping. Teaching our infant to sleep is often our first big parenting challenge, and it's where parents start creating their first set of excuses. "Shhhh.... You have to be quiet, the baby can't sleep if it's noisy out here." "I know it smells a little, but the baby doesn't like it when I change his diaper...."

Beyond the infant stage, "enabling" our children to behave in a substandard manner says that we approve of their behavior. In older children, excusing bad behavior tells children that the world will accept whatever they do as long as they have some excuse or explanation for it. Such excuses can keep children from pushing themselves, and can discourage their motivation toward excellence.

There are often seemingly legitimate reasons why we might excuse bad behavior. These actually teach children what excuses to use with us when they want to get their way. For example, a twisted ankle might become an excuse for two weeks of sitting on the couch and watching television instead of taking out the trash or helping to unload the groceries. At some point, we have to decide when the excuse is no longer legitimate.

JoAnn and I have learned that all things have context and like all children, ours have good days and bad. When they're in the midst of a bad day, we still may need to remind our children that they are responsible for their behavior. Giving them an excuse like, "You didn't get enough sleep last night." doesn't free them from our legitimate expectations. It only allows us to enforce their bedtime with logic later that evening. By the way, children will never admit they are tired.

If a child is behaving so badly that a verbal explanation is in order, I have learned that it's often of value to remove them from the situation before the consultation begins.

It's not very complicated and, once again, we're dealing with the "practice" of parenting – lessons that we learn over time by trial and error. Moving my child to another location for a discussion not only allows me to have their full attention, but allows them to avoid embarrassment in front of other people.

If JoAnn needs to say something critical to me, we have those conversations in private. This arose from our system of values discussion, in which I revealed that one of my father's biggest parenting mistakes was that he'd yell at me in public. I vowed not to do that in raising my children.

JoAnn and I had a procedure in restaurants when our toddler was crying and people around us were glaring. We'd check that his clothes weren't bothering him (A scratchy tag? An allergic reaction to the new soap?) and then we'd attempt to busy him with food, a distraction, or even a pacifier. If that didn't work, we'd remove him from the environment and try to talk him down. If that didn't work, we'd be prepared to say, "If you can't behave, we'll have to take you home."

If the behavior continued, we'd take him from the restaurant quickly and unceremoniously. This is when the serious sacrifice part of parenting comes in, because we had to be ready to leave our meal to teach this lesson. JoAnn really taught me the importance of following through, even when it was ridiculously inconvenient -- and your piping hot pancakes with melting butter and maple syrup had just been put beneath your nose.

Grocery stores are also wonderful locations for "Lifus Interruptus," when you have to interrupt your normal behavior, just to prove a point. On those occasions when our kids would not listen to our requests, like "leave the cans on the shelf," we've been driven to threaten to take them home. On at least one occasion we had to carry out the threat, though we'd just spent the last half hour filling the cart.

MAKING GOOD CITIZENS: A RULE FOUNDATION

I've spoken with some parents who think that teaching their children to be concerned with the opinions or feelings of others might cause them to be competitively disadvantaged, "subservient", or sap their "spirit" and "individuality." We've actually watched some of those children grow up to learn that life goes a lot more smoothly when they are considerate of others. JoAnn and I concluded long ago that we have an obligation to teach our children the Golden Rule.

How do you feel when people with whom you're speaking on the phone allow their children to interrupt constantly? I don't mind a simple interruption for a yes/no question, but when I'm just listening while my friend has a conversation (or worse, a negotiation) with her three-year-old, I often say "call me back when you have more time to talk."

JoAnn and I have had plenty of our own experiences with children wanting to interrupt. At first, we'd respond to simple requests ("Can I have the ketchup...?") But if we were really trying to have an actual "conversation", we realized that we had to firmly lay down the ground rules.

I tended to just say, "Ask your mother." But after a few of those, we had a "system" discussion and JoAnn clued me to a process I hadn't considered. The next time one of our children interrupted, I was now prepared to drop to one knee, look the child in the eye, and point out in a calm and measured voice, "Excuse me, but you are interrupting me, and I am talking on the phone. As soon as I finish this conversation -- which may be very soon -- I will be ready to help you with your GI Joe."

This simple, and serious -- dropping down and looking in the eyes means serious -- conversation allows our child to know that he or she is important, but not more important than the person with whom we are speaking. We clearly didn't ignore all pf our children's requests. Obviously, some situations require immediate action: "I just threw up!" "I have to go to the bathroom!" My mother once offered JoAnn another excellent solution to the interruption situation. She suggested that whenever either of us got home, whether we'd been at the office, the market, or wherever, that we avoid getting on the phone, or emailing, and make a point of spending some time talking with our kids about their day. This simple buffer before starting to make the calls often meant fewer interruptions and more efficiency only minutes later.

Our job is to teach our kids how to live and work within the structure of the world, because as we all know the world is not likely to change to meet their needs. Throughout our parenting journey, we have used our system of regular communication to remain aware of our responses to our children, and we haven't made excuses for their bad behavior. Mostly we've apologized if our kids were disturbing other people, as opposed to getting angry at other people for telling us that our child was disturbing them. We've also learned that a baby crying in a noisy supermarket is not the same as a baby crying in a small restaurant. It's important to pick your parenting battlefields.

LEADING THE WITNESS

Parents can create problems that don't exist because we're desperate to give a name to "what's wrong." Sometimes nothing's wrong. Sometimes our children are just trying to see how we'll react to certain behavior. Having a child throw a tantrum is clearly very frustrating, but it doesn't mean there's anything dramatically wrong. Perhaps he or she just needs a nap or some quiet time.

We've seen some parents, in a search for understanding, "lead the witness" by asking, "Does your stomach hurt?" or "Are you thirsty?" or "Are your shoes too tight?"

Many of these thoughts never would have entered the child's head had we not put them there, and now we're stuck. We've given our child the answer – we've made up the excuse, we've created credibility. Our child thinks, "All I have to do is have a crying fit and tell my mom my stomach hurts and I don't have to go to school." Then he says, "Mom, my stomach hurts." Now we've got to go to the doctor for a reason we handed him. Much ado about a very possible nothing.

One day, while driving to pre-school, Aaron told JoAnn that he really didn't want to go because his "bladder hurt." Aaron was four years old. He wouldn't have known his bladder from his brain. However, he had heard in conversations -- a relative's bladder was a regular topic at the time -- that bladders have problems. So when he needed a medical problem, he blamed it on his bladder. After a brief chuckle, JoAnn explained that she was confident the pain would go away when they got to school. Sure enough, it did. We got a good laugh out of that one when we discussed it at the end of the day.

When I was nine years old, I played Little League baseball. Helmeted, I stood at the plate with three balls and one strike. As the pitch headed toward me, I sensed that it was going to hit me, so I stuck my helmeted head in the path of the ball which, as planned, hit me smack on the helmet. The umpire told me to take my base, but first he stopped the game and asked me if I was OK. I told him I was fine and proudly headed toward first. I had gotten on base.

On my way there, my coach also ran out from the dugout to make sure I was OK. A couple of parents came out from the stands to the fence to check on me. By the time I got to first base, I was crying - not because I was hurt, but because so many people expected me to be hurt.

The key here is that my emotions were driven not by my own feelings, but by the concern of the people around me and their concern for the fact that a pitch had just hit me. As I was crying there on first base, I didn't really understand why. But I realized crying was what I was supposed to do, and at age nine I stood on first base realizing that my emotions could be triggered by the expectations of others.

The lesson I learned from this experience was that my reactions to my children's behavior could often dictate *their* response. As a mother, JoAnn wasn't necessarily "built" the same way as I was. She would always express huge concern for almost any injury. We discussed how to moderate our behavior to show our children that we cared, but at the same time teach them to "walk it off" without feeling sorry for themselves. We vowed to avoid jumping to conclusions or putting ideas into their heads and we worked that into our basic values. We agreed to respond in a measured and reasonable manner to an injury or an accident.

Panic breeds panic. Confidence breeds calm.

It's probable that our children will continue to come to us with excuses, aches and pains. Our job is to do our best to evaluate them in context, and keep mental track of the pains that disappear and those that don't. Consistent complaints require more serious attention, either from us or our doctor, but we need to be careful not to accept everything our child tells us as medical gospel, or to hand them fresh reasons to be hurt or avoid responsibility. The next thing we know our nine-year old will be telling us he can't go to soccer practice because of adult onset diabetes!

MORE DISCIPLINE THAN DISCIPLINING

Over time JoAnn and I have concluded that parenting requires more self-discipline than discipline directed at our children. This is why we continue to spend time defining our goals and touching base about parenting policy. It's up to us to define and apply "the law." If we understand why it's important for a rule to be consistent, and we have the discipline to not make exceptions, our children will not only stay in line, but often anticipate the importance of doing so.

Setting up these expectations becomes a script for behavior. "It's bed time!" usually means brushing teeth is nearby. Emily doesn't do one without the other, and happily points this out to us each night. These expectations make our life simpler too.

Young children need to know how they can please us. By reinforcing good behavior with praise and positive feedback, we can show our children the benefits of living within the rules. I've always been good at criticizing my kids when they were misbehaving. But I was completely unaware of the inverse, which is praising them when they are behaving properly.

JoAnn and I use a number of ways to reward good behavior. The simplest are to tell our kids how proud we are, how much we like their behavior, and to hug, pat, or kiss them whenever they're doing the right thing – whether it's reading quietly, washing dishes, or playing together. These forms of positive reinforcement carry through for their entire lives – and why not? Those forms of reinforcement are still important to all of us! But being positive and loving with children is especially important and effective when they're little.

REINFORCEMENT TOOLS

There are many tools for reinforcing good behavior -- smiles, compliments, kisses -- but most of them are tied to immediate and visible actions. JoAnn and I don't have a lot of rules about ongoing projects like bed making, or feeding the dog, or taking out the trash. There was a lot of acrimony in my childhood home surrounding the "messiness" of my room. I was always being nagged about it, and I really never understood why "my" mess would bother someone else. Nonetheless, I tried to comply, but it was a constant source of friction. As far as JoAnn and I were concerned, it wasn't worth arguing about. I had, after all, learned to keep my room neat because my parents had a neat room, as did some of my peers. As I got older and became responsible for my own environment (my dorm room or apartment), I found I had a peer-driven desire for organization. But none of that was because my parents nagged me every day.

With our very young children, we discovered that one of the most successful methods of long-term reinforcement comes in the unlikely form of charts. Kids love charts! JoAnn, as a trained teacher and an advocate of positive reinforcement, was brilliant when it came to creating progress charts that would allow our children to earn stickers each time they successfully completed a task. My first exposure to the sticker chart method occurred when Aaron was about six years old.

Aaron was and is a sensitive soul. He'd get upset quite easily about the littlest things and his concerns or feelings would too often lead to tears. Noticing that our patience with him was running thin, JoAnn and I decided to create a very simple chart labelled with the days of the week in columns.

Each time Aaron had a "good day," meaning he did not cry or have a meltdown, he would be rewarded with a sticker at bedtime. When rewarded, he would first get to choose the sticker from a collection of his favorite cartoon or television subjects. Then he'd get to stick it on the chart. If he could go one straight week having earned at least one sticker per day, he would get an ice cream cone or the choice of something special at the market. Like beef jerky. (Go figure.)

To my absolute amazement, Aaron began to live for those stickers. Over a period of two or three weeks, he became conscious of when he might have been tempted to cry, and restrained himself. As soon as we were confident that the crybaby had gone away, we suggested that he didn't need the stickers anymore because he was now a "big boy." He bought it. And we had found another arrow to put in our quiver for use downstream with his siblings!

That simple exercise demanded discipline from us, as well as from Aaron. No matter how dumb we thought those stickers were, we had to maintain the attitude, enthusiasm and discipline to keep him interested.

We had to make the chart. We had to place it in his room where he could see it. We had to remind him that his behavior was not going to earn him a sticker at the end of the day, and if we had said he couldn't have one (for crying earlier in the day), we had to follow through - no matter how much he begged or how cute he had been from that moment on. This required nerves of steel!

Aaron needed to learn that if we said he'd lost his chance at a sticker, he couldn't redeem himself by trying to charm us out of it. We had to focus on the greater importance of our big-picture objective, not on the immediate gratification of giving in to our very cute child.

I once encountered a mother who gave her children good stickers for being good, and bad stickers for being bad. Beyond that, at the end of a week, she would add up the goods and subtract the bads and use the total to determine whether her child would get a reward. She didn't understand why it wasn't working, so I suggested she simplify and stop giving the bads, only reward good behavior. Within two days she called to tell me that her kids had become little angels, working hard to get the good stickers.

As I recapped that conversation with JoAnn, we theorized that the motivation to get a sticker is about the sticker, and, good or bad, these kids were getting their stickers. Once it was clear to those very cute kids that the only way to get a sticker was to behave properly, then the desire for the sticker translated exclusively into better behavior.

Learning to play by the rules is a valuable life lesson and it's most easily taught in these very flexible early years. Remember that for most children rules and systems for reinforcement really mean that you care. By expressing our wishes and expecting our children to honor them, we are telling our children that we care about their performance, that we care about the type of person they will become, and that we care about them.

Toddlers long for rules. The sooner you can apply them, the better they'll understand and respect them when they hit their teens. Once, when Aaron was around fourteen and many of his friends were being "grounded" by their parents, he failed to complete a homework assignment. When we got a call from his teacher, JoAnn and I listened carefully. When the conversation ended, we called Aaron into our room.

"Are you going to ground me?" were the first words out of his mouth. It was almost as if he wanted us to prove how much we cared by demonstrating it with a socially acceptable punishment. We asked if he thought it would help if we grounded him. He said, "Yes" -- so he spent the weekend in the house.

Odd as it may sound, I think that grounding gave him some sort of social status, and confirmed there was a consequence for not turning in his homework.

Sometimes the values system of kids is unpredictable. We never had to ground him again.

THE NEED TO DISCIPLINE

As a younger parent, I was often remorseful after criticizing or forcefully correcting one of our children. JoAnn and I would discuss those feelings after the fact, just to reinforce our belief that our objective was to teach some sort of lesson, and to determine whether or not I was delivering the lesson, or over-riding it with emotion or anger. In some cases I probably could have approached the situation differently. In others, we identified the core of the message and re-stated it in a calmer conversation with our child.

There were occasions when we completely disagreed, and that was okay. JoAnn would say I was too harsh, and I would brush her off because I felt as though I was delivering a serious message. Done deal. Message delivered the Dad way. But, if there was an ounce of truth to what she was saying, I would make a point of recapping my anger with our child and explaining why I had gotten so upset in a much calmer, loving way. It's at these times that I remember that my father, after getting angry, would sometimes come sit on the edge of my bed and explain himself to me. He wouldn't apologize, he'd just explain – but that was good enough for me and I loved him for that. I've learned that critiquing behavior, or performance, is best done in the most positive way possible.

With younger children, it's important to communicate dissatisfaction in a direct yet loving way. JoAnn has given me a phrase that allows our children to retain their self-esteem while letting me get our message across. It goes like this: "I love you very much, but I do not like it when you [hit me, hit others, spit, and so on.] My use of this phrase is often followed by swift action, such as immediate transport to their room or some other recognizable consequence.

GIVE THEM RESPONSIBILITY

Around the age of three or four, at the point where your child is beginning to understand your expectations, there is a wonderful teaching opportunity that arises quite regularly. My mother taught us this strategy, and it worked well with our children.

Whenever someone would misbehave in a way that warranted "removal from the situation," we would stop the child, explain that the behavior was not acceptable and define the consequence as being "sent to their room" or "asked to wait outside" or whatever.

After moving the child out of the current environment, we would then say, "When you think you can behave, you are welcome to come back." This puts the child in charge, and even more importantly transfers the responsibility for their behavior to them.

If they returned and continued to misbehave, we would simply say, "I think you may have come back a little too soon. Do you think you should go back to your room and think some more?" Inevitably, they'd either go back to their room, or calm right down.

The need to discipline almost always happens at an inopportune time, such as during your favorite television show or with company visiting. But short-term action -- in this case removal of the child from the group -- communicates long-term goals.

When Emily was in her early teens, I was dissatisfied with the way she failed to greet some guests of mine who had come to our home on business. I made a point of pulling her into the reality of saying hello and then got down to business with my visitors.

I didn't express any anger at that time, because Emily was older and I wasn't interested in embarrassing her. I decided though, that it was important to let her know what my expectations were under those circumstances.

Later that day, Emily was watching TV and I asked her to turn off the TV for a moment. I then explained that I had been "furious" with her earlier in the day because of the way she'd greeted our guests and that, in the future, I expected her to stand, smile, and greet people in our home with the same enthusiasm that I did. I asked her if she understood and she said she did. That was the end of the conversation. No fuss, no muss. Just the facts, delivered respectfully and forcefully.

As parents, we must always think about the long-term results. Those "terrible twos" can one day become the terrifying teens! If we don't apply the energy and self-discipline required to set up our rules and regulations early, our children will look at us in utter disbelief when we try to impose order later on.

THE NEED TO BELONG

Having positive expectations of our children fits directly into one of their most powerful instincts: their desire to be part of something. Showing our children how to live within the framework of our families not only strengthens them, but also prepares them for life in the real world.

Children are hungry for family. Spending time with parents and siblings creates a bond that helps children resist the "need to belong" to other, perhaps less beneficial, groups.

We strive to make our family a "peer group" where our children know exactly how to behave and are always welcomed and respected. In doing this, we have observed that they develop a sense of confidence in themselves and a perspective on their place in the world.

Long ago, when Coby was too young to go by himself, I took him into the bathroom at a local restaurant. When we entered the bathroom the local "beat cop" was washing his hands. I knew this man in blue to be Officer John, so I introduced him to my very young son.

"Coby, this is Officer John."

"Hi, Coby," said Officer John, "Have we met before?"

"No," said Coby, "but I'm one of the Greenberg brothers!" (As if Officer John should have known!)

Officer John smiled at me and told Coby that he was happy not to know him or his brothers too well.

Coby chose his own words in this situation. Although we have established a strong family identity within the walls of our home, neither JoAnn nor I had ever defined "the Greenberg Brothers" as an entity.

In this case Coby chose to identify himself as a member of our specific family group. We had always hoped that Coby would be proud of his family, but we were pleased and surprised to find that he had already woven his identity in with those of his brothers.

JoAnn and I had decided early on that one of our parenting goals was to create a unity among our children. We had discussed what we thought would make them all "stick together." To this day, when one child begins to criticize the other, we do not accept it. We will listen to each side of the story, and then explain that "we do not yell at each other in this family" and that fighting will get them both equally into trouble. Some people believe they should let their kids fight it out. We don't.

Sibling rivalry and family outbursts often require the wisdom of Solomon and significant parental discipline. As our children get older, it may be tempting to jump on the bandwagon and take sides. But it's often our job to offer neutral, objective commentary and to encourage peaceful resolution.

Pushing fair play and honest communication isn't easy. It means you have to stop what you're doing -- writing a book, for example -- and bring peace to the fighting children, no matter how inspired you might have been at that particular moment.

Now... where was I?

THE BEST LAID PLANS

Sometimes when a behavioral problem arises, the "perfect solution" doesn't work out that way.

When Emily turned three we bought her a "big girl bed." We hadn't really thought much about the transition from crib to bed. After all, her brothers had all done it fairly easily.

Thinking about it now, I recognize that over the course of a single weekend we were asking our daughter to go from being held cozily behind bars to being a small speck in a sea of new linens. The transition went very smoothly, as both JoAnn and I had expected. We had scripted the concept of the "big girl bed," and Emily seemed to be adjusting just fine. She slept through her first night perfectly.

During the second night, Emily awoke around 2:00 a.m. calling JoAnn's name. JoAnn went to her side, kissed her, and left the room. That seemed to be enough. Then it happened the next night and the night after. She'd tell JoAnn that she needed to be covered or wanted a kiss.

JoAnn's initial reaction was to teach Emily how to cover herself. At bedtime, JoAnn made a point of showing Emily how to find her covers and how to pull them up. Even after this very careful training, at two o'clock in the morning the lesson seemed to have been lost on our otherwise very resourceful little girl. After about a week, JoAnn confessed to me that she thought that we were helping Emily develop a bad habit.

JoAnn and I discussed the problem thoroughly, and we consulted with the pre-school -- always a good source of data regarding your child's behavior. We concluded that changing beds and beginning pre-school might be causing some kind of "separation anxiety." I typically avoid trying to name the problems my children might be experiencing – as it seems to justify and solidify those problems.

One doctor said that one of us should actually sleep in Emily's room with her. Both JoAnn and I rejected this based on our "Common Sense" override. We chose to try a number of our own brilliant parenting strategies first.

Based on the theory that Emily was suffering from separation anxiety, I suggested, and JoAnn agreed, that we put a photograph of us next to her bed. We took one of our favorite happy couple photos and put it right on her nightstand. I told Emily that if she was lonesome she could look at the picture and that would make her think of us.

It worked the first night. The second night I tucked Emily in, I reminded her that the photo was there, and went proudly back to our bed, secure in the fact that my plan had worked.

Which it had, until two o'clock that morning when JoAnn's elbow wakened me from a deep sleep to answer the call of our lonely daughter.

"Cover me, Daddy," she said in a half-sleep.

I went to her room. "Emmy, you know how to cover yourself," I said sternly, not wanting this visit to be a "sweet" one. "Now go to sleep!" I said as I tucked a sheet around her. "Remember," I said as I walked toward the door, "Mommy and Daddy are right nearby -- you even have our picture to remind you!"

As I left her room I heard her say, "I hate that picture!"

So I went back and removed it semi-spitefully. I took her remark personally -- which, by the way, is a huge parenting mistake. She could not have cared less.

The next day JoAnn took Emily to SavOn to buy stickers and paper for a chart, the "never fail" motivator. The trip itself was part of the process. Emily chose the stickers and she and JoAnn designed the chart. It was titled "Emily's Chart" in large letters at the top with the words Monday through Sunday listed down the left-hand side.

For each night that Emily slept without interruption, she would be allowed to choose a sticker. If she succeeded in amassing a week's worth of stickers, she would get a bigger sticker or an ice cream.

Miraculously, Emily slept through her first night. The next morning she arrived at our bedside dragging her chart and carrying her stickers. After some deep sticker decision-making, we showed her the appropriate day and she placed her sticker. We were sure this would do the trick, once again smug in our belief that we had prevailed.

But the next night at 2:00, same drill. We tried ignoring her calls, but as she continued yelling, we were afraid she'd really wake up. If she completely awoke, it would be harder to get her back to sleep.

Recognizing that interceding while Emily was still sleepy would allow her to fall right back to sleep, JoAnn went in and calmed her with a kiss. We all went right back to sleep.

The next morning Emily showed up at our bedside again, asking if she should go back and get her chart. We told her she had been awake during the night, but she clearly had no recollection of the previous night's events. Nonetheless, no sticker.

This pattern continued off and on for another week. Some nights she'd sleep through and some nights she wouldn't. Every morning she'd show up with the chart and every time she slept through, by agreement, she would earn a sticker. Recognizing that we were now blazing new parenting trails, we tried eliminating naps, we tried earlier bedtimes, we tried later bedtimes. It didn't really matter what we tried. She was still waking up at least five out of seven nights each week. At least, through the use of the chart, she was learning the days of the week. A happy accident!

As JoAnn and I continued to discuss the problem, my biggest concern was that discussing the subject would make it more important than it really needed to be. Emily's inability to sleep through the night was feeding our fears of failure as parents. That was not right. This problem wasn't about success or failure. It was about getting Emily to sleep through the night. Was that a matter of life and death? Not really.

So we concluded that we needed to minimize its importance or we were going to make it larger than life. Making a big deal out of the whole thing might drive us crazy. Even worse, it might create a lever by which our daughter could manipulate us. "You didn't let me play at Amy's so I'm not going to sleep through the night!"

With that in mind, JoAnn and I let it go. If Emmie slept through the night, she'd bring us her chart. If not, we'd comfort her, say no more, and return to bed. We didn't make a fuss and we didn't scold. Sleeping through the night would no longer be an issue. We were just going to wait it out.

It took about two more weeks. Emily was now sleeping through the night. No more calls for midnight tuck-ins, tissues, or reassurance. Ultimately, the solution had been to relax and understand that she'd tire of waking up, or she'd become self-sufficient, or she, too, would just find it in herself to "move on." And that's just what happened. She didn't even care about the stickers once there was no achievement associated with it.

Sometimes it just takes the confidence to know that a certain behavior won't last forever. If it's not something that affects people around you, it can certainly be ignored. We learned that some "problems" can go away if we stop feeding them by thinking of them as problems.

Sometimes, by changing our behavior, we are capable of making changes in the behavior of our children. It takes time, patience, and objectivity. Mostly, though, it takes time.

<u>CHAPTER FOUR SUMMARY</u>

To best APPLY THE RULES...

- We have to apply rules early. It is not only easier, but also a safer starting point for the eventual rule-testing that comes as children get older.
- Reasonable and consistent expectations must be communicated to our children, so that we can build their emotional scaffolding.
- Understand the need for dynamic change. We must reflect regularly on our experience, and communicate with our parenting partner.
- Be willing to revise your plan by using long term values to adapt to specific situations. These conferences and revisions are the keys to resourceful and effective parenting.
- Flexibility is absolutely necessary. Although we, as parents, try to anticipate as many situations as possible, the fact that both we and our children have our own personalities creates a dynamic situation to which we must adjust.
- We, as parents, may need to make sacrifices of our own or put off our immediate plans to instill a point or teach a lesson.

CHAPTER FIVE

RESPECT YOURSELF

"That you may retain your self respect,
it is better to displease the people by doing what
you know is right, than to temporarily please them by
doing what you know is wrong."

- William J. H. Boetcker

RESPECT YOURSELF

JoAnn and I have taught and learned many lessons while parenting, but after all the discussions about making beds, washing dishes, and getting good grades, the most important two lessons we have learned translate to two major values: RESPECT and TRUTH. These two go hand in hand. If our children don't respect us, they're clearly not going to feel compelled to tell us the truth.

In my youth, respect for "elders" was a given. Children rarely "talked back" and were taught to give up their seats on the bus for older people. We were not only made conscious of the world around us by our parents, but also by a society that insisted on norms of behavior from children.

A student who misbehaved in class -- me, for example – could be sent home by the principal of the school, and that student's parents — mine -- would give absolutely no thought to questioning the school. In fact, that young student might be greeted by an angry parent with, "What type of self-respecting young man would do something that stupid?" Being ten years old was not a valid excuse – to, say, my parents.

Today the rules are different, and roles aren't quite as clear: "Kids these days are just different." What's funny about this phrase is that I can remember hearing my parents say it, and I'm sure they could remember hearing their parents say it.

As enlightened as we might think we are as parents, we're just another generation grappling with the fact that things change, children test, and often the answers are not the same as they used to be. We, like the generations before us, are dealing with entirely new concepts: cell phones, video chatting, and personal communication devices that eliminate the need for people to gather in order to interact with each other. I suppose my grandparents felt that the television was revolutionary, and my father was an avid watcher, but in those days performances could not be recorded and replayed. This lack of immediate gratification was, in itself, an important lesson. Our schedule was designed to fit around the national broadcast time of our favorite programs – and if we missed them, we missed them. There was no opportunity for redemption (internet, DVR, etc.) we just had to wait for summer reruns.

So the world now bends to our needs, and the desires of our children. Our society is filled with experts who opine about the psychological impact of allowing our children to play with guns or letting them run around the house naked, or any number of things that have become the anxious territory of today's parent, but early on, JoAnn and I decided that we'd focus on the basics, and that we'd recognize our role as more traditional parents. We'd remain open to the concerns and changes in our society, but we would always fall back on our basic parenting goals and expectations.

We determined that teaching our children respect for others starts with teaching them respect for us. We were confident that this could be done without sacrificing their individuality or personal development.

Recent generations have seen the pendulum of parenting swing from valuing the *collective* toward the growth of individualism. Today, when a child disturbs a classroom full of children, the focus is on why that child is having a problem, or even on whether or not the teacher is doing a good job of maintaining order. The child carries minimal responsibility for the fact that he or she is disturbing the class, because the assumption is that there must be some external factor.

We recently visited the John F. Kennedy Library in Boston and had an opportunity to watch some of his press conferences. Here's how he put it in 1963: "I think when we talk about corporal punishment, and we have to think about our own children...it seems to me, to have other people administering punishment to our own children...puts a special obligation on us to maintain order and to send children out from our homes who accept the idea of discipline. So I would not be for corporal punishment in the school, but I would be for very strong discipline at home so we don't place an unfair burden on our teachers."

Today, some parents not only believe that their children should be exempt from reasonable cultural behavioral expectations, like sitting quietly in class, but often display no regard for the education, feelings or comfort of the other kids in the class! What lesson does that teach their children?

In 1963, the importance of the teaching the entire class out weighed the problems of a student who was interrupting, and that was the prevailing attitude with regard to the role of teachers and the responsibility of parents.

We were recently at a garden party attended by a group of close friends and families. One family had brought their new seven-month-old Labrador puppy, who was naturally the center of attention for all the children.

As I watched the kids play with the dog, I noticed one little boy who seemed to have a particularly rough approach to the puppy. When he did something a little mean, he looked around to see if anyone was watching. About an hour after noticing some of those behaviors I was talking to a friend when I saw the little boy lift the puppy aloft by its tail. At that moment, I moved toward the boy and loudly said, "Put that dog down! How would you like it if I lifted you up by your tail?"

The little boy dropped the puppy and went running into the house crying in search of his mother. Within moments, people started telling me that I had no business scaring that little boy and intervening where his parents should have. There were other critiques, including many that agreed with my actions but thought I had been a little harsh. I agreed on both counts. That was a lesson his parents should have taught him, but I could not stand by and watch him hurt the defenseless dog. His father, with whom I went to high school, came out and asked me not to speak to his child like that. I could only say "Someone should – the puppy couldn't."

In earlier generations, parents rarely blamed another adult or made excuses like a sleepless night, too much sugar, or a scary political climate to excuse the behavior of their child. Bad behavior was simply unacceptable, and having a "stranger" correct your child's behavior in public was often an enormously humiliating yet valuable lesson for both parent and child. Parents not only understood the clear-cut differences between right and wrong, but they also took responsibility for their children's behavior. As a result, the children were expected to behave properly, and parents felt that input from another authority figure was more beneficial than embarrassing.

How can we make our children responsible members of society? How can we teach them to think about more than just themselves in a world in which role models include bad sports, porn stars, drug users, or social freaks? When celebrity is defined as success, and getting noticed is the most important thing, how do we install the "R" (for Respect) chip in our kids?

One way is to teach them to respect the people who made their lives possible. That's us, their parents.

My parents raised me to believe that, under most circumstances, they knew what was best for me. I was to respect their knowledge by accepting their instructions and behaving accordingly. Often this meant being "seen and not heard."

It seems a little harsh, but when one of my kids insists on talking at me while I'm on the phone, I totally understand why it made sense to teach me to listen as well as to talk. Childhood is a time for learning, and a lot of learning occurs when watching and listening. It makes perfect sense for parents to apply a philosophy that promotes the concept of listening to and observing the needs of others.

How did you learn to keep quiet? How did you learn to say "please" and "thank you"? Did anyone ever encourage you to give your seat up to an older person or to hold open a door out of courtesy? Do you do these things now, and do you believe that this is the best way to teach your children to do the same? Although old-fashioned, each of these simple acts carries a deeper message of respect for others:

- Learning to keep quiet means I am not the most important person in the world, and that we need to be sensitive to others.
- Learning to say "please" and "thank you" teaches our children that there is a formality to the manner in which we address each other.
- Giving up one's seat is a measure of courtesy and a lesson in anticipating that the feelings or needs of other (and older) people are important.
- Clearing our table at a fast food restaurant teaches our children that the people who will need the table next are worthy of consideration.
- Putting the shopping cart back at the market is a great job for an eight- year-old.

All of us are capable of doing these things. By modeling them, we can teach our children that these behaviors are important to us and should be important to them. Children are keenly aware of how we, as parents, treat those around us, like food servers, grocery store checkers, bank tellers, and hundreds of other people we meet in the world.

Each of us has heard some wisdom from the past regarding parenting. It was once widely believed that if we spared the rod we would spoil the child. Although the use of a "rod" is not acceptable these days, the need for consequences is crucial to communicating the do's and don'ts of everyday life.

Our children need to know that we have expectations of their behavior. The fact is that they LOVE this. It lets them know where they stand.

To teach children respect we must show respect for ourselves. It's not easy to live an exemplary life, but that's exactly what being a parent is. None of us is perfect, but we each have little opportunities to show our children the high road not only in our expectations of them, but in our expectations of ourselves. Simple things, like swearing a lot -- a tendency I had to battle for many years -- or parking illegally, become behavioral norms for our children.

Some of these things are just habits we've formed as adults. But during the time in which our children are most impressionable and their moral and emotional scaffolding is being built, we have to be conscious of the lessons we're teaching them.

How can we expect our children to respect us if we behave in a manner that is contrary to the lessons we are trying to teach? Some people justify this by saying to their children "Do as I say, not as I do." Unfortunately, in most cases, kids are going to DO as their parents DO and not listen to what their parents SAY. We must believe in our knowledge and through our behavior create the moral world in which we want our children to live.

That's what developing the culture of our families is all about. It isn't easy, and it often requires repetition, but in the end it's essential and worthwhile.

THE POWER OF SUGGESTION

As I think about my own role as a parent, I notice that much of my behavior has been subconsciously influenced by what I saw my father do. Each night when he came home, he would go directly to a sink and wash his hands. As it turns out, I find that my first act upon arriving home is also to wash my hands. It didn't start as a conscious imitation of my father, but as way of washing off the outside world and coming to the family ready for a clean, new start. I suppose it was the same for him.

When I was younger, and he and I were walking down the street, we would inevitably encounter someone less fortunate than we. In every case, my father would be kind to them, perhaps giving them some change, and then lean over to me and say, "There but for the grace of God go I."

Recently I have found myself doing the same with the same explanation for my children -- and something tells me that they'll be doing the same with theirs. There is no subtlety in this; it is, and was, a simple expression of gratitude to something greater than ourselves. A lesson learned through simple words.

Many of us have learned the Pledge of Allegiance: "I pledge allegiance to the flag of the United States of America, and to the Republic for which it stands, one nation under God, indivisible, with liberty and justice for all."

I'm not sure I really understood the true depth of its meaning when I was nine years old, but I definitely knew how to recite it. As I've gotten older, the words have much more meaning for me, and I'm grateful to be a U.S. citizen. That set of words, and my reverence for them, was implanted in me as part of an everyday routine during my elementary school education. It became a comfortable recitation, a time when everyone did the same thing, in unison, out of respect for the flag and our country.

With the Pledge in mind, it occurred to me that there were certain phrases, "implanted recordings," that might become part of my children's internal communication system.

Let's call this process "scripting." Scripting also applies to matters that are as mundane as answering the telephone. No one at any job ever gave me instructions about phone-related etiquette. I learned it all at home. I was instructed to answer cheerfully -- "with a "smile" in my voice -- and to say, "Greenberg residence." We didn't have an answering machine, so I was also taught how to take a message. These skills came in very handy when it was time for me to find an entry-level job in the real world, but I learned the script at home.

When I feel as though my overt messages are not getting through, this sense of subconscious communication really gives me hope. I sense that even if my children aren't willing to do something "my way" now, at some time in their lives, they will know what to do from the subconscious behavioral and verbal scripts that I have placed in their minds.

Recently I was offering advice to Aaron as he planned to rent a truck and move furniture to a new apartment: "Put the heaviest stuff closest to the cab." I said, to which he replied, "I know, Dad. I'm your son." I got a smile out of that.

Although I can't really guarantee this idea about implanted suggestions, I can tell you that I find myself drying my feet by flapping them with my socks (as my father did), tapping my wedding ring musically on the steering wheel (as my father did), pushing myself to try things that I'm afraid of (as my mother did), and getting really serious and telling my children that I love them at the strangest times – just as my father did any time, or anyplace, completely out of the blue, and sometimes even immediately after a punishment.

Scripting worked with me. It has worked with many of my friends who were rather rebellious as kids, and I believe it will work for most people and their families.

KID PRO QUO

We were once expecting visitors from out of town. We had told Aaron that they were bringing their teenage niece with them. We had also told him that we were expecting him to help her feel comfortable.

When the fateful day came and they arrived, Aaron was hanging out with a group of his friends.

I sought him out and said, "Our guests have arrived. Please come and meet Jeannie."

His response was, "They're your friends, Dad, not mine."

Although I was upset by that comment, I stayed calm and asked him to join me away from his group of friends.

Once clear of the friends and in a relatively private situation, I held his shoulders firmly, stared directly into his eyes and said, "Understand this, dear son: If what is important to me is not important to you, then what is important to you will not be important to me. And, at this point in your life, you need me -- for a ride to baseball practice, for example -- much more than I need you."

Aaron immediately grasped the concept and said, "What do you say we go say hello to our guests." As it turned out, the niece was really cute and Aaron ended up very happy with his decision to help out. Things your children resist often turn out quite nicely for them. It's important to remember these positive outcomes so that they can be cited downstream when resistance raises its head again.

LYING

As adults, most of us have recognized that lying is a losing proposition. By the age of twelve most of us have been embarrassed by some sort of fib, whether it was boasting of a manufactured success with a female friend, getting a phantom "A", or having finished a homework assignment that somehow never got turned in. I also remember that whenever I found myself telling a lie, or being caught in a lie, a little voice in the back of my head was telling me it was wrong. For that, I felt slightly ashamed, and I learned that lying and self-respect are linked.

My parents put a premium on truth and JoAnn and I have tried to continue that tradition. Nonetheless, like their father before them, at some point or other our children, like all children, have tried to slip one by us. I caught one of my kids trying a classic Greenberg maneuver.

"Have you brushed your teeth?" I asked Coby.

"Yes."

"Oh, really? I didn't even see you go into the bathroom."

(Pause.)

I can remember as a child telling my mother that I had brushed my teeth when I hadn't. Slightly suspicious, my mother walked calmly into the bathroom and returned with my dry toothbrush. "How did you brush your teeth without getting your toothbrush wet?", She asked calmly.

History repeated itself.

Like my mother, I emerged moments later with the dry toothbrush. My mom hadn't made a big deal of it, and neither did I. But the jig was up, and two generations had proven to their kids that parents are not dummies and that it was going to require a lot more imagination to put something past us.

Beyond the compulsory lecture about truthfulness, our message in this instance was that even the simplest issues, when lied about, require serious preparation and planning. In this case, wetting his toothbrush would have taken Coby about the same energy as actually brushing his teeth. Lying was going to require a lot of forethought. He realized that it was a rare occasion when one could actually get away with it. Telling the truth was simpler, easier, and the right thing to do.

Children lie for the same reasons we do: They are unhappy with the truth, so they make up their own version of reality - or they've done something wrong and they fear that the truth will get them in trouble.

Our approach to our children "re-writing reality" is to give them a non-judgmental opportunity to talk truthfully about the parts of their life that they would most like to change. Maybe they don't want to say that they hate the guitar, or that a sibling hurt their feelings. Maybe they're hiding shame because of something a friend did, or maybe they're afraid that we won't understand.

Whatever it is, JoAnn and I have let our children know that lying about reality doesn't make it different. We let them know that we love them in their real world, whether Daddy lost his job, or Mommy and Daddy had an argument. To de-personalize the discussion, we remind them that they should be sensitive to their friends who might also lie for similar reasons.

Regarding children who are afraid of getting in trouble, my parents taught me a brilliant approach. Their secret weapon was called an "Armistice." I learned this word when I was about six, and I had always thought that word was theirs – but, ultimately, it came in quite handy when the word arose in vocabulary tests.

When I was growing up, if I broke a piece of furniture or did something that I knew was going to get me into a lot of trouble, I knew I could go to my parents and ask for an "Armistice." This meant that, if approved, I would not be seriously punished.

It also meant that we were going to have a really long and deep conversation about how the event occurred, and how it could best be avoided in the future. Kind of like appearing in court.

The catch was that when I would ask for an Armistice, my parents would respond by saying, "Maybe." Then, they'd listen to me explain what boneheaded thing I had done just before their ruling. They never exploded in anger, never double-crossed me by saying after the fact that the Armistice wasn't in effect, and never made me regret having told them the truth.

As I got older the Armistice went away, but the habit of being truthful, and the concept of honest confession and reasonable response remained. This allowed me to be a bonehead and still maintain my self-respect. Recognizing one's mistakes, owning them, and learning something from them builds character.

JoAnn and I were in complete agreement about this. Neither of us is particularly punitive, but we both understand the importance of taking advantage of the teachable moment to make our point. It's inevitable that our children will test the boundaries of our gullibility, but the Armistice is a very good way to give them a safe approach to being truthful -- and once the truth is out, the seeds of mutual respect are planted and it's a relief for all concerned.

THE PINT-SIZED POLYGRAPH

Most children have their own built-in polygraph machines. They are extremely intuitive, and can see right through adults who might be trying to buy them off or misdirect them. Sometimes, even when we're being truthful, our kids are capable of discerning things, emotions or fears that we may be trying to hide. Children have incredibly powerful antennae.

When Emily was three, JoAnn was due to have surgery. It was a long-planned procedure that would require hospitalization for three days and two more weeks in bed. Although we had told our older children about it, we had decided not to tell Emily until the weekend before the Monday surgery.

The previous Thursday, despite the fact that no mention of the subject had been made, Emily asked JoAnn, "Mommy, what would happen if you couldn't pick me up from school?"

Here was three-year-old Emily giving JoAnn an opportunity to smoothly segue into an explanation of what we knew would be the procedure for the coming two weeks. JoAnn told Emily that she was going to go to the hospital for an operation, and explained that Emily's big brother, Aaron, would be taking her and picking her up from school. Emily reassured JoAnn that she would show Aaron where to sign her in and she later told Aaron she'd be on the swings when he came to pick her up.

It was almost as if Emily was trying to make the situation easier for JoAnn.

You may be asking why we chose to not to tell Emily about the surgery right up front. First, we didn't want her to obsess about it and ask too many questions. We learned this lesson when Aaron was three years old, and we told him that his Mommy was going to have a baby in seven months. Seven months is a really long time in a child's life, so when Benjamin finally arrived Aaron had asked so many questions that he probably knew enough about childbirth to enter medical school!

With the next children, we didn't reveal JoAnn's pregnancies until much later. If they had noticed anything or asked questions, we would have happily answered with the truth. But seven months, we learned, is a lot of waiting. Patience is not a virtue with which children are often endowed.

The other reason we chose to withhold information about JoAnn's surgery is that medical problems and hospitals are a bit scary to everyone, especially children. We wanted to minimize Emily's opportunity for anxiety. I know that I'm often more anxious about a business meeting during the days that precede it than I am during the actual meeting. Giving Emily too much time to think about the surgery would have given her time to get scared. This way the event came and ended quickly: "Mommy went to the hospital for three days and now she's home."

Because children are so perceptive, the delay in telling Emily also minimized the possibility that we might reveal our own fears and anxieties in front of her. She'd definitely have noticed.

This is where the idea that children are pint-sized polygraphs comes in. Having these little students studying us full time is a very compelling motivator of good behavior as a parent. Because our children "mirror" us, and are smart enough to see things about us that we may not see, it's important to create an openness when our kids are old enough to express their observations.

A vivid example of how perceptive children can be came up one evening at the dinner table when, after a very long, disappointing week, and many years of toil in one particular job, fourteen-year-old Aaron said, "Hey Dad, if you hate your job so much, why don't you just get another one?"

"What makes you think I hate my job?" I asked, trying not to reveal my surprise.

He replied, "You're a happy and funny guy, Dad, but lately you don't seem so happy and funny."

I guess he'd figured it out.

What's worse is that he was right. Within months, I resigned from that position and moved into a more satisfying situation. I will never forget that Aaron not only recognized my pain but encouraged me to do something about it. He even offered to "cut back" and spend less. He was willing to do what he could to help me get happy again. He was essentially reminding me to respect myself, and to practice what I had been preaching to him.

Kids can sense the difference between false praise and real praise. If we tell our children that everything they do is great, it cheapens the meaning of really doing something special. This prevents kids from knowing where they really stand.

A few years ago, I saw Emily hastily scribbling a birthday note for me moments before the family gift presentation. When I started reading the cards (in no particular order) I noticed the other boys notes were nice, and Emily's was textbook sweet, but not particularly thoughtful. Coby, however, had written me an extraordinarily thoughtful and loving note, and I made a point of thanking him for it with real gratitude. "What about mine Daddy? Didn't you like it?" asked Emily. "Of course I liked it Emily, but you didn't put nearly as much thought or concentration into yours as Coby did." Basically, I called a spade a spade – and now I get truly thoughtful notes from my daughter too. Calling our kids out keeps them honest – and teaches them how to be honest without being mean.

CROSS-PROMOTION

In teaching respect, it's very important that we show respect for our partner. To help my children appreciate their mother, whenever possible, I tell them how lucky they are to have a mommy as wonderful as theirs, and how well she takes care of them. Through this process, we lovingly joke about her; her sense of style; her navigational skills (or lack thereof). I never criticize or bad mouth her and I often explain to them how hard she works to make all of us happy.

As a result, our children have developed a sense of appreciation, and a point of view about JoAnn as a person, not just their mother. In the long run, this approach lets them see her as an adored individual for whom they have compassion and a thorough understanding. In the short run, these conversations give our children a warm feeling for their mom and the security of knowing how much I love her. They learn that loving someone means complimenting or defending them, even when they're not around to hear you do it.

My children have said -- and JoAnn has confirmed -- that she does the same for me. When I perform simple tasks around the house, I sometimes hear my wife tell our kids that I am "the world's greatest fixit man" and that our house would fall apart without me. Clearly, this is an exaggeration, but at least JoAnn knows how to keep me working around the house.

CHILDREN AS TENANTS

The primary job of parents is to raise children who, when pushed from the nest, are able to fly. But when they fly away, who does that leave in the nest?

When Emily was fourteen I picked her up after dinner at a friend's house. She was explaining to me that the family she had been visiting operates in a manner similar to ours. She said they laugh hysterically around the dinner table, they take turns talking, and they're fun to be around. I asked her, demonstrating my desire to "promote" my love for her mother, "Does their Daddy love their Mommy as much as I love yours?"

Without missing a beat she said – "Yea – he's just like you – he treats her like she's his wife, not just like she's the mother of his children."

"Wow", I thought, what a brilliant way to describe what happens in some relationships when children come along.

Let's review that: "He treats her like she's his wife…" That must mean that he treats her like he's still attracted to the woman he wooed and married - the woman he respects, as he did at the time of their marriage, and with whom he presides over the activities in their home. And, hopefully, the woman who still prioritizes private time with him whenever possible.

The second part of Emily's wisdom -- "not like she's the "mother of his children" -- clearly means that she's seen couples where the wife has gotten lost in her devotion to their children and whose attention to the children consumes all of her time, including discretionary time she might have previously spent with her husband.

Someday our children will be gone. As a result, we need to maintain our individuality, our separate lives and interests, so that when our kids move out we have something more to talk about. In this way, we don't just become Mommy and Daddy holding an empty bag. Not only that, unfortunately, I can say in all candor that husbands need wives, and if their wives are simply the "mothers of their children", they're likely to look elsewhere for someone to fill the wife void.

JoAnn and I have adopted the theory that our children are tenants in our relationship. They are renting space from us, and sooner or later we expect them to be out on their own. Of course, we love them very much and we let them know that as often as possible. But parenting includes taking time for ourselves. We want our children to know that we had a relationship first, and that we don't expect them to be our dependents forever.

Years ago, when we took Aaron to college, we had quite an eye-opening experience. For JoAnn, it was the culmination of a six-month crying spell. For me, as I watched him unload his possessions (his "stuff") in his dorm room, I was reminded of my own departure from home and the little trinkets that I had carried from place to place -- just as he now carried his Dodger autographed baseball and his Webster's Collegiate Dictionary.

I was watching my child have an experience I had already had. Here we were dropping our oldest son off in the "real world" to see if the lessons we had taught him over eighteen years were going to work. Both JoAnn and I knew he'd survive his freshman year. We knew that he wouldn't starve and that he'd make friends. We just had to sit back and let him start to fly. We had to have confidence. We had to respect him and his decisions. It was easier for me than it was for her.

Aaron had the tools we had given him, was meeting his new roommate, and was optimistic that he and the complete stranger in the other bed (with equally doting parents) would live together in this shoebox of a room like long-lost buddies. He was ready and, I suppose, so were we. The lessons we had taught him from age two had now become the foundation for his way of life. He was out of the nest.

Weeks later, the news from college was that he had succeeded in becoming friends with his roommate. He had found the student store. He had even managed to feed himself on numerous occasions. Lessons about friendship that had started when he was a little boy had all come into play: conflict resolution, sharing, listening, and understanding that the feelings of others were equally important as his. These lessons had allowed him to slide gracefully into his new unprotected world.

Although we missed him terribly, deep down we were really quite proud.

I have learned that the best way to teach children to respect others is by creating perspective. One of the simplest ways we can do this is by demonstrating to our children that they are not the center of the universe, a common misconception among three-year-olds. As parents, we can teach children the value of privacy. Our children know that there are definitely times when Mommy and Daddy just need to be left alone or times when Mommy and Daddy go out to dinner or to the movies. These times are important to us. Being alone with each other is important to us. Making our relationship a positive, communicative place where we can find refuge from everything, including our children, is important to us.

By respecting ourselves and prioritizing our needs as an adult couple, we teach our child that their needs may be less important than those of others at any particular moment. A failure to do this may lead to the complication of a child who controls your schedule, your emotions, and, essentially, your happiness. Children aren't prepared to wield that much power, and typically, the anxiety they get from having the power causes them to get angry at parents who put them in this position.

This anger sometimes manifests itself as temper-tantrums, abhorrent behavior, the withholding of bowel movements, and so on. Each of these actions is a message; a way in which your child is trying to communicate something more sophisticated than his or her ability to otherwise do so.

On a more selfish note, we've learned that happy Mommies and Daddies make for happy children. Even though you're sometimes forced to impose your will upon your "tenants," they need to understand, respect, and observe that you are fundamentally positive people. People who are willing and able to make a judgment call based on being separate, adult participants in their own lives.

The keys you use to remain happy in a complex world will be carried by your children when they leave the nest. In time, they will use them to guide their choices and define their own goals. As a loving force in their lives we praise them as often as possible, and we let them know that we have standards for ourselves and that we push ourselves to meet those standards. Let them see that you are happy with your own achievements. Praise doesn't come easily from your children, but when they tell you that they are proud to be your child and start telling you what you've taught them, it feels really good.

If your children see you as a happy person in a happy relationship, chances are they will want to imitate you.

CHAPTER FIVE SUMMARY

To better RESPECT YOURSELF...

- Define respect through parental modelling, "scripting," and "cross-promotion," so as to guide our children's behavior and feelings.
- Make children aware of the feelings and needs of the people around us. Simple acts – like being kind to restaurant workers, putting away the grocery cart, or cleaning up at the fast food restaurant, teach children that there are others in the world.
- Have clear expectations that let kids know where they stand: "If what's important to me isn't important to you... then..."
- Live The Golden Rule.
- Collaborate with your mate to present good examples for your children. Show how being truthful is safe, how a reasonable discussion encourages fair resolution. Yelling is not a tactic.
- White lies are lies nonetheless – minimize using them because children will use them too.
- Create a mechanism like the "Armistice" for safe truth-telling.
- Be honest with children. It is the best way of earning truthfulness and respect from them. Try to anticipate possible questions and confer with your partner regarding your unified position. "How do we explain Cousin Larry?"

CHAPTER SIX

TEACH IN ALL THINGS

"I talk and talk and talk, and I haven't taught
people in 50 years what my father taught by
example in one week."

- Mario Cuomo

TEACH IN ALL THINGS

For JoAnn and me, a primary parenting goal was having respectful children and I've addressed the process by which we arrived at our rules for achieving that goal. We created a system of parenting in a positive, but not necessarily permissive way.

In this chapter, we're going to focus on being teachers. I will share with you a few valuable tricks of the trade that I have learned over the years. Some of them JoAnn and I discovered ourselves, and some were given to us by others.

There are an infinite number of lessons to be learned (and perhaps taught) in our roles as parents. These are just a sampling of things that we've leaned on for support during the process, and that we've ultimately found useful.

90/10- SHARING THE LOAD

When JoAnn and I got married, we were told by a wise friend that marriage is not 50/50. It's 90/90. We'd each often feel as though we were giving (or doing) more than half of the relationship's work and, if we could accept that fact, our marriage would sail along relatively smoothly.

After more than thirty years, JoAnn and I agree that the theory remains accurate. The workload shifts. Sometimes I'm doing more and sometimes she's doing more. While raising children, the same sort of flexibility is required. When it comes to our relationship with our children, the scale changes over the years.

In the beginning, we do virtually 100% of the work. We change diapers, we feed, we entertain, and we worry. Our infants and toddlers, on the other hand, spend almost all of their time observing, and smelling, and tasting, and learning. Although those things don't help the laundry get done or the sheets get changed, they're doing their jobs too, as nature ordained. That's just the way it is.

When you find yourself feeling like you "do everything around here," know in your heart that if you did a good job, your kids will come around and carry their own load someday – like, as soon as they can drive.

GENEROSITY / GRATITIUDE

Parenting demands a tremendous generosity of spirit, but as our children get older we are can teach them to help us so that things aren't quite so lopsided. At a certain point, we can enlist their aid by saying things like, "Please help me clean up your toys," or "Sit still while I put your socks on." Narrating and naming these tasks is an important part of the process, as we are actually teaching our children how to do these things for themselves. "First you prepare the sock, now you put it over your toes..." At some point, probably when you're in a hurry, your child will want to do it for himself. If you're in a hurry, try to explain that he can do it next time and reward him for his patience. If not, guide him, encourage him, and reward him with praise (and maybe even a phone call to someone else who would be proud.)

Whenever possible, and sometimes out of the blue, JoAnn and I would make our children aware of the world around them.

"That's an interesting building, isn't it?."

"Look at those pretty flowers. Nature is so amazing!"

"We're so lucky to have...a nice home...a safe school...warm clothes...food... good health...."

We all live in our own circumstances, but the more we teach our children about the ways in which they are fortunate, the more perspective they'll have regarding their place in the world. Adults are able to disconnect themselves from some of life's ugliness, such as mean people, terrible news headlines, or even Cousin Gab-a-lot who calls and talks for hours because he or she is so lonely. Our children will undoubtedly be exposed to these aspects of life. It's important to use exposure to these events as contrast to their lives so that they can see, and we can teach them, first-hand, the many reasons that we all have to be grateful.

Gratitude can be taught through example. Show children the charitable things that you do, and point out how these acts are charitable. For example, I am a regular blood donor. When our children were young, I would often take a child with me, just to show how important I felt it was to do something for others – even if it wasn't fun or easy. Our children also join us in other charitable activities, such as packing food for the homeless or clearing brush from neighborhood hillsides.

This awareness that we as a family are helping others creates a very strong bond for all of us. We have found that getting involved in the community not only enhances our self-worth and gives our family a positive reputation in town, but also expands the hearts of our children. We're not the most active people in our community and we don't overtly seek out these types of opportunities. But when they arise, we take advantage of the occasions to get involved and set an example.

By teaching our children to appreciate what they have - including our mate, our home, our car, their grandparents, their school, the blueness of the sky, and so on - they will ultimately come to the conclusion that they must owe the world (and perhaps us) some sort of gratitude. JoAnn and I didn't consciously plan this, although it has proven to be correct with our sons, all of whom, upon leaving home and going to college, realized the "service" void in their lives. Now they have to shop, clean, and do their laundry. No one's there to hug them when they are sick, no one helps them with the ugly tasks of splinter removal or drain clearing. Suddenly we started hearing "thank you" for our decades of hard work.

Teaching gratitude has a dual purpose. It makes kids aware of the beauty they can find in simple things, and it also keeps their egos in check. We talk about beauty in Nature because, as important as we may all believe we are, when we examine and appreciate the sheer magnitude of Nature we gain a perspective that keeps us from feeling we are more important than everything else. There isn't much that is man-made that compares to the beauty of a flower, a full moon, the taste of a pear, or the power of the ocean.

JoAnn and I often remind our children that there may be many people in the world with more than they have, but there are also many, many, more people who have less. It is important to understand what it means to be rich in love as well as in things.

Today, television shows us images of people who, we are told, "have it all" -- millionaires, actors and actresses, all of whom make a living in a world of make-believe. Not surprisingly, our children tend to believe that this is how life should be.

In addition to selling us myths of happiness, we're also bombarded with advertising that is designed to make us want more -- whether it's a new Mercedes, a vacation to Disney World, or just a beer. This pressure to consume creates a pressure to compare. However, nothing compares with the value of a strong family and loving relationships between parents and children.

PATIENCE

Like flowers in our gardens, children often bloom in cycles. But that doesn't mean that we only care for them when they're blossoming. JoAnn and I have found that there are times when one or more of our kids will be slacking off, or behaving selfishly and, just at the moment we're planning to address their behavior, they will suddenly become angelic. It's as if they have a sixth sense, and this sixth sense is their ability to "read" our emotions – which can only come about if they've learned to feel and assess the feelings of the people around them.

LOVING EQUALLY – 100 % MAXIMUM LOVE

I have a friend who feels that her little brother "stole" all the love and affection that her parents had previously been giving to her. Sibling rivalry is an age-old problem. However, as a result of the way she felt as a child, my friend dedicated herself to giving her own first-born preferential treatment. No matter how you look at it, by treating him differently, she created the same situation that she complained about in her childhood.

Ironically, my friend -- whose child is now old enough to go to therapy with her -- explained to us recently that she was shocked to hear that because he was always treated differently, he felt separate from his siblings and not like part of the family.

The effort she had made to single out her son had been successful. Unfortunately, it backfired and became a self-fulfilling prophecy.

JoAnn and I believe in what we call "100% Maximum Love" for those who qualify – and our children automatically qualify. Typically, the group also includes aunts and uncles, grandparents, and a few lucky individuals whom we consider honorary family.

Recipients of Maximum Love have no need to compete for "favorite" – because everyone is the favorite. When I have been asked by one of my children, "Who do you love more?" I reply, "I love you all equally -- the maximum." When I am asked, "Who is your favorite?" I say, "You are all my favorites."

Maximum love really simplifies family life and allows us, to completely avoid that whole "How much do you love me" battle. When we asked our third son, Coby, if he knew how much his mom and dad loved him. He said " "You love me as big as the sky."

He was absolutely right.

RITUALS AND ROUTINES

Another part of family life that gives our children a strong sense of identity is participating in family rituals.

First, we eat together every Friday night. This ritual began years ago when I was deeply immersed in my work, going to the office and staying until all the work (for that day) was done. I remember looking forward to listening to radio dramas in the car on the way home. Of course, the radio dramas ran from eight to nine pm, so it was pretty clear that I was spending far too much time at the office.

After a few months of this, my heretofore-patient wife asked me, "What time do you think you get home from the office?" Innocently, I went into deep thought and said "Eight?" "Not so," she said and produced a short chart she had kept proving that my average return to the homestead was at approximately 9:15. I had a long commute!

With chart in hand she made two simple demands: "From now on, you will come home for dinner by 7:00 on Friday nights."

"Okay."

"And, you will only work one Saturday a month. Okay?"

"Okay."

From that day forward I made it home almost every Friday night by 7pm to enjoy a sit-down dinner with my family. That was the beginning of a ritual that we learned to love and depend upon. As the years passed, one night per week often became three. At this point, it takes a lot to get me to miss dinner with my family. Our dinners include an expectation of good manners, and scintillating as well as "privileged" conversation.

The good-manners expectation means we sit together, put our napkins on our laps, ask people to pass various items, wait to eat until everyone is served, and so on. Basically, this is an opportunity to train our children so that they will behave properly when they go to dinner elsewhere later in life.

Privileged conversation means that we have a stated understanding between all family members that what is discussed at the table remains within the family. It is not discussed at school. It is not used to tease. It is to be respected. Establishing this enforced level of trust between family members has united our children and given them a bond that comes from keeping and sharing personal and confidential information. Nowadays, when we remind them that something is confidential, they give us the "duh" look.

If someone betrays a dinner table confidence, there is a very stern conversation about it. We've learned that it can take a little time for the trust to develop, so no one gets grilled in the third degree. Mostly, dinner is just enjoyable, honest family chat – a far cry from the inquisitions that were the dinners of my childhood.

I play softball on Sundays. It is one of my rituals. Over the years, my children have come to the games, acted as batboys, ridden their bikes, begged me for snow cones, or gotten a Slurpee after the game. They know it's Sunday, they know I'm playing, and they know they're welcome to come along. Each one of my sons has enjoyed participating in the ritual and now my daughter does too. She loves to come to the games, watch our personal belongings and, at age fifteen, babysit the children of my teammates.

At a time when JoAnn and I had our hands really full, my mother, who believed that children should get to know their cousins, hosted dinner for the entire extended family on Monday nights.

As a result, my kids are very close with their cousins and, as they grew older and capable of driving, they still made it a point to come to "Monday Night Dinner." They even brought friends after asking Grandma for permission. It was a brilliant tradition and lasted until they were all in college and poor Emily had to have dinner with all of us old folks. Now that they've graduated from college, the cousins all remain very close. When the family gathers there is an immediate closeness in the next generation. We really enjoy that they, too, feel and behave like family.

These regular activities become a predictable framework for our lives. My father used to take me with him to buy the newspaper every Sunday. I take my children to softball games. We share a special dinner every Friday night. As my children have grown, I've noticed that these shared activities are footholds that keep them solidly grounded as various forces try to shove them off balance. Most importantly, these shared activities make us a family.

PICKING YOUR FIGHTS

My parents fought with each other, my sister, and me, about everything: whether we made our beds, whether we ate our vegetables, who was the 10th President of the United States, how much longer we would be in the car if we were going 60 miles per hour and Fresno was two hours away. This left a lasting impression on me, which I took to my marriage and parenting.

As a family, we spend no time arguing over disputed facts. We just look them up. This is different than my upbringing, where uninformed but absolute opinions were proffered daily. Today, on the rare occasions that I, the Father, am proven incorrect, I apologize properly and console myself with the fact that I am setting a wonderful example of contrition and humility.

Arguments based on observations, or interpretations by others including "he said / she said" are immediately dismissed for lack of "provability." These discussions, when they have reached their most obnoxious stage, are called a draw. No winner, no loser. Peace is the most valuable commodity in our home.

FAIR TRADE

If we don't fight about hair, food, or music, what battles do we fight? The following is a list of rules upon which our expectations are based. So far, so good. But any of our children who don't live up to these rules can expect some feedback.

- We expect them to do what they say they'll do.
- We expect them to tell the truth.
- We expect them to call when they're going to be late.
- We expect them to respect our desire for privacy, or quiet.
- We expect them to participate with us when asked.
- We expect them to be nice to each other.
- We expect them to respect their elders and teachers.
- We expect them to be considerate of others.

If they do what we want, they can dress and wear their hair however they'd like.

Seems like a fair trade to me.

By the time we get to serious issues, like wearing too-short skirts, caking on eye makeup, or getting pierced in strange places, this groundwork of good values allows for decisions that will be synchronous with our expectations. If they are not, we'll know we did our very best and were true to ourselves and our values.

CHAPTER SIX SUMMARY

To TEACH IN ALL THINGS...

- Don't "keep score". When your kids are very young, you may have to do everything. That may be logically impossible, but it's what your daily experience will be so be resigned to it.
- As you do the tasks at hand, teach your children how to do them themselves. Gradually, slower than the proverbial molasses in January, they'll begin to take over some of that work.
- Create routines that become recognizable and predictable for your kids. Refer to the steps of the routines using the same words and phrases. The routines themselves are powerful teaching tools. Your children will be gratified to know that somebody actually knows what's supposed to happen. At first that somebody will be you. Eventually it will be them.
- Point out the uniqueness and wonder that's present even in everyday experiences. The trees, the clouds, the way one person helps another to cross the street. Everything can be an experience of discovery. Something can be learned from everyone.
- Lots can be learned from spirited family discussions. Nothing (or nothing good) can be learned from fights. Asking really good questions is often more enlightening than providing answers. Some of the best questions have no answers at all.

EPILOGUE

"Our greatest glory is not in never failing, but in getting up every time we do."

- Confucious

EPILOGUE

Even if we can learn from all these lessons, and we work diligently at being loving and reasonable parents, there are significant variables in our children and their environment. These situations, contexts, and personalities require us to continually adjust in order to shape the unique people that our children are now and will become in the future. When we give them strong foundations, we will see them evolve before our eyes.

Writing this book has revealed to me that being a parent gives me the opportunity, pleasant or not, to sit down and scour my life looking for the origin of certain emotions as they arise throughout the process. Continuing today, I find my parents surfacing in me in all kinds of ways. Some good, some not-so-good, but I'm lucky to have created, through my family, relationships with people who love me enough to reflect back at me the negatives and positives of my ongoing behavior.

Today my sons relate to me in a manner that is not only joking and playful, but also sensitive, loving, and understanding. It's as if they are my greatest fans – as

I am theirs – but we still manage to have some very frank discussions, sometimes ending in apologies for things said in the heat of battle. This is truly the payoff for standing firm in your own values throughout their upbringing. Yes, there were times when I was stern, seemingly unfair, or resolute – but at this moment it's clear to me that the lessons of my parental failings were as valuable to my children as those of my successes.

In many cases, peers, "society" and "culture" will step in and teach our offspring a thing or two. I've seen it happen. I've watched my kids learn difficult lessons and come out of them just fine. I've seen broken hearts, professional disappointment, and personal confusion – and that's just in me! Most importantly, I've seen every parenting situation end with the amazing result of more mature, more tuned-in, and more loving human beings on both sides. I guess we've just got to love and teach them as best we can, and, in turn, they will continue to love and teach us.

In watching our children wander off into the sunset, we just need to know that we have given them the tools necessary to adjust, adapt, and succeed in each successive environment. That's the job.

I hope that you can take the lessons of this book and make them work for you as they have for me, JoAnn, and our family. Next to having chosen the right mate, being a parent is truly the greatest pleasure in my life.

People often say that their child is a gift, and that's true. But the biggest gift you can ever give your child is to be loving, caring, and firm parents who show them the way. Teach your children and they'll teach you.

Eventually the birthday parties will be less elaborate, the trips to the beach will be less frequent, and the football games will be watched elsewhere. You and your partner will be left as you began, happy to share each other's company, but with a lot more stuff to talk about.

Good luck, and have fun.

ACKNOWLEDGMENTS

Dedicating this book to JoAnn is one thing. Acknowledging her contribution is another, which should be clear in the preceding pages, and for which there is not enough space to do justice. Additionally, I couldn't have been a father, or written this book without the commentary and understanding of our four incredible children: Aaron, Benjamin, Coby, and Emily. As test subjects, they have flourished in the lab, and for that we are all truly grateful.

My parents had a friend, Archie Hurwitz, who was an artist. If someone would ask him how long it took him to paint a specific painting, he would say "My whole life." Well, that's how it is with this book; a gathering of thoughts and feelings that began the day I became aware of my surroundings.

I learned quite a bit about parenting from my parents, whom I must thank for setting such solid examples. They are gone now, but I see them every day in the values of my family and children. Of course, their parents, my grandparents, who lived much harder lives, set the earliest examples of resilience and perseverance.

My sister, Jan, taught me that sentences should end, and has always been a wonderful co-conspirator and steadying influence. When the chips are down, my sister is always there.

Neal Halfon has been my champion for a number of years. His fine mind and professional perspective kept driving me deeper toward the simplest conclusions and observations. Mitch Sisskind was fated to be my Editor. We met once, years ago, before the book was ready... and then rejoined efforts when it actually was. Mitch's clear sense for plain talk makes my words more precise and easy to read.

My friend Tom Nolan and I decided one day that our efforts in raising children were actually a form of healing the wounds associated with the way we had been raised. Jim Milio had kids when I wrote my first draft, and, as a result of reading it, decided to raise them "The Greenberg Way", which gave me faith that this could be communicated. Susan Leon, one of my earliest advocates, allowed me to believe a book could be written, and Matt Cooper had enough faith to put his money where his mouth is. Dr. Ron Pion taught me about the "would-be learner" and Phil Savenick is happy that I'm me... even if he's not like me. Lincoln Caplan II published when he was very young, and I thought that was cool, and my friend, Harold Koh, and his siblings were, as a result of either Korean tradition or parental whim, given sequential middle names, which I noted bound them together and motivated the alphabetical naming of ours.

There are various others - family, friends, and professionals - who contributed time, notes, enthusiasm, talent, and meals toward helping me get these thoughts organized. They include: The Rosin Family (especially Karen who did some fine-tooth combing for me), The Jonas Family, Rabbi Steven Carr Reuben, Cantor Chayim Frenkel, Dr. Alan Yellin, Marty Nislick, Phil Oderberg, Barbara Clark, Christopher Horner, Patsy Ihara, Cynthia Jacquette (cover design), Marni Kamins, Sandra Kulli, Laine Kontos Oberst, Andrew Solt, Karl Epstein, David Shambaugh, David Holtz, Linda O'Toole, Tom Seder, Sharon Goldinger, Gay Harwin, Carole Ann Zappia, and many others over the years who have shared their stories and lessons.

Among the others along the path, I'd like to thank all those who believed in me, counselled with me, and helped me understand their processes. This includes people who chatted with me, shared their techniques, and generally talked about their love for their children, as well as those strangers whose behaviors I merely observed.

I am also truly lucky to have the benefit of wise counsel from good friends, and to have attended Verde Valley School where I learned to embrace cultural differences.

And finally, my newest allies in the publishing and publicity worlds. Thanks to Nancy Greystone (Communicating with Clarity), as well as Gareth, Oren, and Aga at Authoright, and Daniel and Kate at New Generation Publishing. I appreciate your patience and professionalism.

CPSIA information can be obtained at www.ICGtesting.com
Printed in the USA
LVOW13s0823221013

358022LV00003B/285/P